Toddlers:
an instruction manual

Toddlers:
an instruction manual

A guide to surviving the years one to four (written by parents, for parents)

Joanne Mallon

NELL JAMES PUBLISHERS

Published by Nell James Publishers
www.nelljames.co.uk
info@nelljames.co.uk

British Library Cataloguing-in-Publication Data
A catalogue record for this book is available from the British Library.

ISBN 978-0-9567024-4-9

First published 2011.

The Publisher has no responsibility for the persistence or accuracy of URLs for external or any third-party internet websites referred to in this book, and does not guarantee that any content on such websites is, or will remain, accurate or appropriate.

Note: The advice and information included in this book is published in good faith. However, the Publisher and author assume no responsibility or liability for any loss, injury or expense incurred as a result of relying on the information stated. Please check with the relevant persons and authorities regarding any legal and medical issues.

Printed in Great Britain.

Contents

Acknowledgments

Thank you to all the parents I've coached, interviewed and corresponded with, and who have contributed to this book. Thank you to everyone who took the time to write down what they wished someone had told them about toddlers.

Thanks especially to Katie Lee for asking me to write an Agony Aunt column at AOL's *ParentDish*, which opened my eyes to the extent to which toddlers have the capacity to fox their parents. The questions sent in about under fives outnumbered all other subjects many times over, which led me to think that there was probably a book's worth, and more, to say about the subject.

Thanks also to Linda Jones at *Ready for Ten* for asking me to specialise in writing about children's behaviour, which never stops being fascinating.

Thank you to Alison at Nell James Publishers for agreeing that the world has got space for another book about toddlers.

Thank you most of all to my family for your support, especially my partner John Higgs and our children, Lia and Isaac. Thank you kids for not going too feral whilst I was writing and just for being so fantastic in every way.

Introduction

When I told other parents that I was writing a book about toddlers, most of them rolled their eyes and said 'Well, there's certainly plenty to say about THAT!' And then would come the stories – the broken nights that left them weeping with exhaustion; the terrifying temper tantrums that descended without warning; the potty training that went on for months; the poos in inappropriate places.

I have been a journalist for 15 years, a parent for 12 years and a life coach for 10 years, all the time talking to mums and dads about the challenges that life throws at them. And I think toddler-dom is one of the toughest stages of childhood for both parent and child. There's just so much going on, and neither of you really knows how to handle it. Toddlers are often unfairly branded as the 'Terrible Twos', as if this is all they're about. In fact many children can be complete angels at two and right little devils once they hit three. And others seem to sail through this stage trouble-free (though brace yourself, they're probably saving it up for the teenage years). But however your child handles this stage of their life, there's a lot more to them than being terrible. Let's not forget they can be terribly lovely as well.

So that's where I hope this book will help – I've spoken to hundreds of parents and gathered their stories, tips and advice to help you now. Many of the parents I spoke to were already past the toddler stage, so they could look back with the benefit of hindsight and give you the best of that experience – the stuff they wished that people had told them at the time.

Whether your child is not yet a toddler, or has already entered The Whirling Dervish Years, I hope you find some help in the form of this book.

You will see that many of the parents quoted in these pages write their own blogs to document their family lives and I would encourage you to visit their sites and say hello. If you need a support team for your toddler troubles, here they are. I've collected the addresses at the back of the book so do go and visit their websites if you want to talk to any of them. Being the parent of a small child can be exceptionally lonely at times. But the great thing about being a 21st-century parent is that you can easily reach out online and know that you are not alone after all. So have a read, make a new friend and be inspired. You never know, you might want to start a blog yourself.

Think of this book as the start of the conversation rather than the last word. None of us knows it all or would even pretend to. Use the ideas you find here to help you make up your own mind about what is right for your child. Because the only parenting expert here is you – even if you don't really feel like you know what you're doing. To be honest, most of us feel like that. We're all really just making it up as we go along. Just don't tell the kids.

If I had to sum up the parenting approach of this book, it's basically relaxed, with boundaries. We don't sweat the small stuff, but we're big on please and thank you. It doesn't matter if you wear the same green T-shirt for a week, as long as you go to bed on time. Choose to leave your tea if you want, just don't bite your brother instead.

But first – what is a toddler? In this book we are referring to children aged from over 12 months up to nearly four, when they may be close to starting school. You will probably have read developmental checklists that tell you what your child is supposed to be doing at various ages, but try not to get too hung up on these. Every child and every family is different – it's all normal. Some children are walking before they turn one. Others stay on their bums long enough to get you worried, then they get up and dance across the room. Some are incorrigible little chatterboxes from the word go, others barely utter a word and then suddenly start speaking in sentences at three. It's all fine. It's all good.

Whilst I would urge you not to panic if your child hasn't reached a particular developmental milestone, do talk to your health visitor or GP if you have any concerns. And don't be afraid to go back again if you don't feel you've been properly listened to the first time. A parent's instinct is a very powerful force, so if you feel there is something wrong then ask for help. But don't worry if your child isn't doing exactly what his or her peers are doing. Chances are he or she will get there in the end.

And although inevitably we will be looking in this book at the tough side of life with a toddler, we know that it's not all bad. Your toddler is a gorgeously squidgy bundle of love, interested in everything and learning something new every day. Take pride in everything they achieve. They might drive you mad at times, but you wouldn't be without them. As they start to speak, you'll hear the sweetest words imaginable. The toddler stage may be infuriating at times, but it'll be over in a flash. So savour it. You'll miss it when it's gone.

My own children are now eleven and eight. I can see now how the seeds of their personalities that were emerging when they were toddlers have continued to grow. My daughter could be an angry toddler, prone to fantastic, dramatic temper tantrums where she would arch her back right out of the pram. And now she wants to be an actress. It figures. My son was, and continues to be, a placid person. He's interested in the world, but likes to know what's coming next and prefers to follow a routine. It's as if their toddler selves were concentrated versions of the people they are growing up to be.

At the end of every chapter I've included some thoughts from parents about why we love our toddlers. Because whilst we may be considering whatever gawdawful way our under fives are tormenting us – whether it's refusing to eat, sleep or stop biting their pals – we can't lose sight of the love. Whatever the little munchkins put us through, we still love them with all our hearts and wouldn't be without them for anything.

I would like to dedicate this book to two toddlers whom I love very much. They aren't with me anymore. One of them is now at secondary school and the other one is nose deep in a book – my lovely daughter and son, Lia and Isaac. I never thought we'd get this far. Love has seen us through.

Joanne Mallon, October 2011
info@joannemallon.com
www.JoannetheCoach.com

Chapter 1: Threenager alert

Meet the Threenager – AKA the teenage terror in a two foot body. Utterly convinced that the world revolves around them, unwilling to take responsibility for their actions and a constant drain on your energy and resources. And yet also more than cute enough to be able to get away with it.

Toddlers can be so much like teenagers in all but age, so why do toddlers behave the way they do? In this chapter we're looking at:

- What is going on in those little heads?
- Why is it making them so angry? Surely moodiness wasn't due for another ten years?
- What's the best way to communicate with a toddler?
- Why do toddlers play favourites?
- What's so great about toddlers anyway?

I'm sure you've heard the phrase 'Terrible Twos' and perhaps you assumed that age two was where it would all kick off with your child. And maybe it will. Or equally, you might sail past two with no problems and it might be a case of 'Terrible Threes' or 'Fearsome Fours' instead. They could even start giving you the evils from around one.

Either way, if you get past the toddler stage with no real displays of challenging behaviour, then brace yourself for the teenage years because they're obviously saving it up for then. There are so many similarities between teens and toddlers, hence the term 'Threenager'. Both are apt to get stroppy for no good reason that their parents can understand. Both are prone to strange sleeping patterns. Both may complain loudly about the food you serve up. And just when you've had enough, both may redeem themselves with a winning smile and a flash of loveliness.

Typical toddler behaviour

So the delights that Toddlerdom has to offer include:

- Mood swings – your toddler can go from tears to giggles and back again in the blink of an eye;
- Lack of control – 'wow, that baby looks so tasty I think I might bite him';
- A fascination with everything – there's so much to learn;
- Boundless energy – a full night's sleep is for wimps;
- Frustration – the source of many a tantrum.

Basically, a toddler is like the worst boss you ever had. But cute. Sorry to keep harping on about the cute thing but it is important. That and the overwhelming love. Some days they'll be the only things that get you through.

And tough as this stage may be for parents, it's not exactly one long picnic for your toddler either. Every day brings something new to master – language, social skills, where to pee, weird green things to eat. And then stuff like new siblings or starting nursery rock your world as well. It would make anyone's lip wobble.

But we're in this together, parent and child. Just don't forget which is which and you'll be fine.

Why I love my toddler

'I love my toddler because watching him discovering the world is like seeing things for the first time. You can almost see the connections being made in his head as he finds yet another fascinating thing and works out what it's all about. He approaches everything with a huge appetite for fun and adventure. Watching a daddy-long-legs jumping about was, unaccountably, the funniest thing.

'I got down onto his level and, yes, from his viewpoint this thing was hilarious with its huge spindly legs. He insists I sing and dance around the kitchen with him standing on my feet like it's the most im-

portant thing for us to be doing. And, when you stop and think about it, it probably is the most important thing for us to be doing.'
Ellen Arnison
In A Bun Dance, bundance.blogspot.com

Don't fear the challenge: embrace it
Challenging as toddler behaviour may be, don't be scared of it. It might not be as bad as you expect. You may find that your inner reserves will get you through. You may locate a good spot in the wardrobe to hide until the worst of it is over. You can do this. You will do this. And remember to take some snacks and your iPhone into the wardrobe with you when you go.

There's a very wide spectrum of toddler behaviour, all of which counts as normal – for some, tantrums are a daily occurrence, whilst other children barely raise a peep. Some children happily enjoy a wide range of food, whilst others are more likely to throw their dinner on the floor if it contains the tiniest speck of the unknown. Some children will display all of the characteristics above, whilst others very rarely do so.

If you feel your child's behaviour is substantially out of kilter with their peer group, then do speak to your GP or health visitor for advice. Trust your instinct if you feel something's wrong. But remember that the range of normal toddler behaviour does include many things which parents find very undesirable. This too shall pass. And at least by the time they hit the teenage stage you won't have to potty train as well.

Things I wish someone had told me about toddlers
Josephine Middleton is a mother of two who writes the award winning *Slummy Single Mummy* blog:
'The important first rule of parenting toddlers, which you must remember at all times – they are Not The

Same As Us. You know the book, *Men from Mars, Women from Venus?* Well toddlers are in a whole other solar system. If you thought men were messy, selfish, unreasonable and infuriating, then you've got a big surprise just around the corner when your adorable baby learns to toddle...

'Toddlers touch everything. Absolutely everything. To avoid permanently having to put books back on shelves and pick up bits of broken crockery, the safest things to do is not have anything at all smaller than a coffee table below waist height in your house. This might look odd, but it will save you hours of bending.

'Sometimes toddlers are cute, but only to you, their parent. If you don't have young children of your own, other people's toddlers are just incredibly irritating, like a small yappy dog that isn't yet house trained. What does this mean for you? It means for a few years, your regular friends will do their best to avoid you. It's nothing personal, it's just what happens. To make sure you don't end up spending every afternoon wandering alone around town, breaking up the monotony by taking your toddler to an Asda cafe for a "treat", you need to get some mummy friends. This isn't always easy, and may involve a few torturous mornings scouring the local toddler group, but finding yourself a like-minded mum who can share your hell is absolutely imperative.

'Trying to encourage your toddler to eat a range of wholesome fruits, vegetables and pulses is very admirable. It is also almost impossible to get them to actually swallow any of it. The cheapest and quickest solution, and the one least likely to end in you scraping full plates into the bin whilst you mutter under your breath "I don't know why I bother, I may as well just come home from the supermarket and empty the carrier bags into the bin", is to just cook beige foods. Young children really only like beige foods. Think bread, pasta, potatoes, cheese, chips. Possibly banana if you strike it lucky.

'To avoid having a house full of horrible plastic toddler toys, don't buy your toddler toys. Simple. Everyone knows toddlers just like sticks and bits of cardboard and stuff anyway. And you can spend the money you save on wine, which I always found added a lovely rosy edge to the end of a day with a toddler.'

Josephine Middleton
Slummy Single Mummy
slummysinglemummy.wordpress.com

Communicating with your toddler

The really key aspect to communicating with your toddler is to always remember that they can usually understand much more than they can say. They're also pretty nifty at responding to the atmosphere around them, however calm or stressed that might be.

So your child has the words in their head, but just can't get them out. They'll be able to soon, but just not quite yet. And even though they know what they want to tell you, you might not fully understand, or think they mean something else. Can you see how frustrating that might be for a person? Little wonder that toddlers are prone to tantrums.

How to talk so toddlers will listen

To a little kid, you the adult can be pretty imposing (whether you mean to be or not) simply because you're so much bigger than they are. Therefore if you want to ensure that your toddler takes in what you're saying, it can help to get down on their level and look them in the eye when you're speaking to them. It's a simple thing but it really does make a difference – it makes a welcome change for the child who may be more used to hearing your instructions boomed from on high. Obviously it's not always practical to do this, and you might get arrested if you tried it whilst driving down the fast lane of the M4, but give it a go when you can.

The other advantage of speaking to your child on their level is that you won't have to shout (nor should you, unless your intention is to frighten the child). If you can feel yourself veering into shouty parent mode too much, getting on to your child's level is a good, calmer alternative.

Communication strategies for parents

* It can help to hold your toddler's hand as you speak to them – the aim is to slightly still their naturally physical nature and help them concentrate on what you're saying. Also it may prevent them from running off if they don't like what they hear;
* Use simple, straightforward language that your child will understand. This doesn't mean you have to boom in single syllables like a children's TV presenter. But think about the language you use and the concepts you take for granted and ask yourself – will my toddler really know what I'm on about?
* Keep it direct and don't over-explain. They don't have to know every why, when and wherefore of the fact that it's time for bed;
* Be aware of your own tone of voice. Do you sound hesitant, like you don't really believe what you're saying? Do you phrase commands as if they're a question ('Why don't we start getting ready for bed now?'). Toddlers will pick up on this hesitancy and crush you like the mini-tyrant they are. So practice a firm and clear tone of voice. You're going to need it.

Chattus Interruptus

Some parents feel that when your child wants to talk to you, any other conversation you may be having with other adults must cease immediately (mid-sentence if necessary), as you drop down to your child's level to find out what they want. Those who do this usually justify it with a 'He/She won't wait'. But how will he/she ever learn to wait if you don't give them reason to?

One defining characteristic of toddlers is that they live life very much 'in the moment' – whatever is happening right now is much more important than what went before and what's coming next. Patience is a skill that takes a long time to build and it is a rare toddler who has it naturally. Sometimes it is children who aren't the first born in the family who tend to be most patient, simply because the natural order of things means that they've always had to wait their turn.

Similarly to how you deal with tantrums (which we'll look at in detail later in the book), how you deal with situations like this sews the seeds as to what sort of adult your child will become. So if you want them to grow up thinking that the world revolves around them, go right ahead and react immediately.

If you want your child to wait a little (perhaps whilst you finish your current conversation), one method you can use is to encourage them to hold your hand when they want to speak to you. You can gently stroke their arm or hand, which tells them that your attention is on its way. And if that doesn't work, pick up on the cues from your child and make plans to skedaddle.

This is one of those topics that can really divide parents, but I am of the opinion that it's never too early to learn manners and think of others. Also I think cultural differences can come in to play – in some families, loud raucous conversation with everyone speaking at once is the norm, whilst others are much quieter. So be sensitive to the situation you're in and encourage your child to do the same.

What worked for us – Backpacks and trust
Writer Emily Carlisle has twin toddler girls and an older son:
'Once twins get active it becomes really hard keeping tabs on them, especially once they decide they're too grown-up for a buggy! Backpacks with reins are a brilliant way of keeping them close to you, but we also found that a little trust went a long way. We abandoned our buggy altogether before the twins were two and they've got great road sense now.'
Emily Carlisle
morethanjustamother.com

Why has my lovely child turned feral?
Children of all ages, but particularly toddlers, are like a barometer of the world around them. So if your child's behaviour changes, and especially if it becomes more chal- lenging, the first place to look is the rest of their world and ask yourself what this is a reflection of. Reasons for changes in toddler behaviour could include:
• The arrival of a new sibling;
• Parental arguments or separation;
• Tiredness – especially if sleep has been disrupted or you're in the process of dropping the daytime nap;
• Pressure to potty train before they're ready;
• Moving house;
• Change of key worker in nursery;
• Any kind of stress at home.

This is particularly true when there is stuff going on in a parent's life that takes their attention away from their child – you've gone back to work, so Junior suddenly starts waking up at 3am. It's all about gaining your attention.
And whilst it can be distressing to see how your child picks up on the undercurrents of life that you thought you'd

protected them from, at least it makes it easy to see what is going on and to change whatever needs to change to stop it from continuing.

Ditch the guilt

Please don't feel guilty or start blaming yourself if your child starts acting up as a result of stress at home – these things happen in all families and once you start feeling guilty as a parent you might never stop. It takes up way too much energy and probably gives you wrinkles as well.

In fact, I think it's one of the loveliest things about toddlers that their external world is also embedded within them, etched right through like the writing in a stick of rock – a toddler will never pretend to be happy when they're not. Adults could learn a lot from that.

> *I wish someone had told me to go easy on myself*
> 'The one thing I feel quite strongly about now is that I wish I'd cut myself a bit of slack – especially when I had three daughters under four and a half and was trying to work from home part-time. I spent a lot of time worrying about whether I was doing the right thing and in some ways always wishing them onto the next stage (ashamed to say because I thought it would be easier – it's not!). At the time it feels like all of the baby feeding / bottom wiping / toddler tantrums go on forever but actually it doesn't – I wish I'd realised that instead of feeling so sorry for myself. The toddler years are precious – your children need you and every day they discover something new, and you act as their teacher / guide / interpreter to understanding the world – the tragedy is we don't know those years are "golden" until they are over.
>
> 'If I could go back in time I'd tell myself that it's unrealistic to do everything perfectly by the book

(organic veggies, Suzuki violin at two, no trash TV, no sweets except Fridays) – sometimes you just have to get by and just do enough. Sometimes you will lose it, shout and pretend not to hear when they cry and that doesn't mean you've failed – just that you're a human being who gets tired and sometimes needs a minute to herself. I sometimes look at old photos and notice I look exhausted and glum – maybe if I hadn't been so hard on myself I would have enjoyed those years more. I remember those years being really tiring but full of love and joy too.

'I would stay away from competitive mums too – look beyond their four-wheel drives and there is often emptiness. I'd also scrap most of the toddler activities – they were for me not them and all I did was get stressed rushing from one to the other when we might have been better just kicking through autumn leaves or hanging out at a friend's paddling pool. Developmental milestones are just another thing to beat yourself up about – what's the rush? They all get there in the end!'

Jo Waters
Health journalist and mother of three
jowaters.co.uk/blog

Was it something I ate?

And of course, don't forget the effect of food on your child's behavior. As they encounter more and more different meals, you may find that some foods and additives do produce a marked reaction. I'll never forget the first time my two year old encountered Spaghetti Hoops. She started bouncing around the living room as if she were a human hoop with extra batteries. We started noticing that anything coloured orange was inclined to set her off – orange juice in particular could only be given with caution in a wide open space. Over time this effect has become much less marked, but realising that it was happening was a real help in working out exactly why she literally couldn't sit still at times.

Is it all your fault?

The reasons why your child behaves as they do are a mixture of their genes and the environment in which they are brought up. The only one of these elements that you can have an effect on is their environment so it makes sense to focus your attention there.

There are elements of your child's personality that will stay with them their whole life, from the day they are born. But it is how we, as parents, treat our children as people that makes the crucial difference.

Don't believe the hype

There are many surveys and studies done into how and why small children behave as they do. Take everything you read of this ilk with a very, very large pinch of salt. For whatever a survey says, there will very likely be another survey along in a few months to say the exact opposite. As one claims that nursery turns children into little hooligans, so another trumpets that nurseries are great for confidence building. Meanwhile, if you're the parent who has no choice but to use a nursery, it's easy not to know which way to turn, apart from straight towards 'Guilt City'.

Talk to other parents as much as you can. If you are despairing about your child's behaviour, you may find that they're a little angel compared to some.

Always look for the positive aspects of your child's behaviour and praise them – the time they shared or played nicely; when they've walked along without running off, or made a good effort at their lunch. Every child, even the most challenging, has got good qualities and these are what you want to nurture. Your child will see that this is what earns them the attention they crave and the positive behaviour will continue.

I wish someone had told me not to take it personally
Journalist Heidi Scrimgeour is a mother of two boys with a close age gap:
'My boys are 21 months apart and my youngest walked at nine months so I felt like I had two toddlers on my hands for about four years! I definitely struggled with the toddler years. My eldest didn't exactly have tantrums but he was very headstrong and could be excruciatingly defiant.

'In particular I tended to take his behaviour too personally – I remember an occasion when I was pushing him and his brother up a steep hill in the double buggy and he kept taking his crocs off and dropping them out of the buggy on purpose, making me have to keep walking back down the hill to retrieve them. In exasperation I eventually let him believe I was leaving them behind and then of course he screamed all the way home in protest. You'll never win a fight with a toddler.

'Irritatingly, I miss the toddler years now and when I'm around my friend's toddlers I'm struck by how cute and funny they can be – but at the time it's hard to see that. I wish I had taken it all a bit less seriously and made more time to laugh at the absolute insanity that is toddler behaviour.

'I think, especially when it is your first child, being confronted with classic toddler behaviour up close and personal for the first time can be really bewildering. What might have seemed sweet or funny in other toddlers you've encountered before becomes quite stressful in your own. And because they're programmed to test every boundary, say "No" more than any other word and it can feel almost as though they're deliberately winding you up. That's what I mean by taking tantrums personally – it's easy to assume they're seeing how far they can push you and of course they are, but not for personal reasons – just because that's how they learn. If you have the capacity to embrace that learning experience with them then the toddler years can be hugely rewarding. And I'd say enough time to yourself to recharge is vital for anyone spending extended time with toddlers!

'The pre-verbal stage is especially hard with tantrums – they know their own minds so clearly but lack the words to say what they're thinking – baby signing helped at that stage but it's not for everyone. Just remember this too shall pass.'
Heidi Scrimgeour
www.heidiscrimgeour.com

Playing favourites
Even if you do manage not to take it personally, what happens if your threenager shuns you, and makes it very clear they'd rather have someone else instead? Andrew Watson is an actor, author of two parenting books and dad of two under fives. He's found that it is not all bad if your child starts playing favourites:

'One disadvantage of your child's growing ability to express themselves is the possibility that they begin to display a preference for one parent over the other. That was certainly the case with my daughter – although she was very happy to be alone with me, if there was ever the option of involving mum, I'd be banished immediately. It even got to the point that I'd helpfully retrieve an out-of-reach toy, only for her to insist on my replacing it so her mum could get it down for her instead.

'Such explicit favouritism is perfectly normal for toddlers. Often they gravitate towards their main carer, or the parent of the same sex. Alternatively, they may want whichever one seems to offer the most stimulation or comfort. And sometimes it's just because they're looking for a reaction.

'Though such behaviour can be hurtful, it helps to understand the motivation, and to focus on the positives. By playing favourites, your child is exploring their relationships, displaying a growing ability to verbalize thoughts and feelings, and learning to influence and make sense of their environment – however unbalanced that sense may be.

'And ultimately they must be pretty secure in your love to feel they can so flagrantly abuse it. In response, you and your partner must be united and establish clear limits on what your child can and can't command. If you're the one who's spurned, do all you can to rise above it, overcoming their rejection with quality time and consistent and unconditional love. If you play it right, you might find you still get the cuddles, but your child won't let you anywhere near the nappies!'

And Andrew feels that toddlers have much to recommend them:

'Despite the bad press, toddlerhood can offer parents an enormous amount of enjoyment and satisfaction. For some fathers in particular, the toddler years are the time when parenthood ceases to be something that's tolerated and starts becoming instead something to be relished, when at last they're able to interact and get something back.

'It might be exhausting running after your toddler all the time, but with their new found mobility comes an independence that's rewarding to witness. Then there are the first flashes of a sense of humour. And even the exasperating moments, from a refusal to eat dinner to a determination to repeat the same old bathtime routine over and over, can be a source of satisfaction as you begin to appreciate you're raising not just an automaton that needs feeding, washing and resting in an endless cycle, but a distinct human being, full of whimsy and preference.

'The toddler years are special, as your child wants to go it alone yet still needs the regular reassurance of your presence. As a result you get to watch them flex their independence and develop a distinct individuality, while still wanting regular cuddles and comfort. And, thanks to their increasing ability to express themselves, you can be sure – unlike when cuddling a baby – that they're quite happy about it.'
Andrew Watson
www.awwa.co.uk

I wish someone had told me that toddlers are the best
Ursula Hirschkorn is mum to four boys and thinks that toddlers are far more terrific than terrible:
'I know it is wrong to have favourites, but I can't help it, my favourite age by far is two. Of course it is the age more usually prefaced by the word terrible, and often with good reason, but it is also quite terrific too.

'You see for me people don't really come into their own until they learn to talk. Babies are cute and all but all that gooing and gurgling doesn't do it for me, even stroppy answering back is better than the dumb insolence of a newborn. I remember being terrified by the blank eyed stare of my firstborn son. I was convinced I had birthed the next star of *The Omen* and combed his tiny body for the mark of the devil.

'But by the age of two I can't get enough of my chubby little angels. As the twins sprout new vocabulary every day their latest trick is to take me around the house David Attenborough style, giving me a wide eyed guided tour of the mundane. Everything they see they gasp and point at exclaiming its name with the same wonder the BBC reserves for a hitherto undiscovered sea creature or the coupling of some near extinct mammals.

'Zach went through the contents of his entire toy basket, pulling everything out, holding it aloft and declaiming its name. "Rocket", "plane", "choo choo train", "honey toast" (note to self, must get around to tidying that thing out).

'Developing language has enabled Jonah to give full rein to both sides of his slightly divided nature. In Hyde mode he may utilise his new skills to shrill out demands or refusals, increasing the decibels the longer it takes you to respond.

'At breakfast time he will start with a polite "Chinamon baggie pleath" (he has a slight lisp), asking for his usual morning repast of a plastic bag full of *Curiously Cinnamon*. Should you ignore him for a moment or two while attempting to feed the children who actually have to get out to school though and he will start to screech the same sentence over and over again at the top of his surprisingly loud voice.

'However, just as you are about to put him out with the bins after the millionth demand, he will switch back to Jekyll and sing out "Lub you mummy", his squidgy little face wreathed in smiles as he reaches up for a cuddle. Cue mummy's heart splashing into a puddle at his tiny feet.'

Ursula Hirschkorn

fourdownmumtogo.blogspot.com

Key points about Threenagers:
- They're a lot like teenagers, only smaller;
- They want all of your attention, and they want it now;
- Changes in your home life can easily affect your toddler's behaviour;
- Get down on your child's level to talk to them as much as you can;
- Even though it may feel like they're trying to wind you up on purpose, never take it personally;
- They drive us mad, but we love them really.

Why I love my toddler
'If there's a thing to not touch, my son will touch it, a thing not to be done, my son will do it. And guess what? He's the only one. All the others play nicely and heed their parents. My little boy? Seemingly not. And this has worried me. Why isn't my son like other children?

'I've realised when my son misbehaves in public, which is becoming rarer to be fair to him, he isn't being terrible. He's just being terribly normal. Even the iccle baby Jesus probably mucked about in his dad's workshop, and touched a plane or a chisel that he shouldn't have. My son is testing boundaries. He's pushing limits and seeing how far that can get him. He's exploring. He's learning. And, rather than being an embarrassment or worrying about it, I have begun to think that it's beautiful to see. The only thing he has against him is that he's got a dad who worries too much and guess what? I'm learning to relax a bit.

'So what if my son isn't like other children? That's just how I like it.'
Spencer, a stay at home dad
sahdandproud.wordpress.com

Chapter 2: Sleep solutions

If anyone had dared to suggest when my children were born that they'd still be waking up at night when they were past two, I think I would have lamped them (the commenter, not the children – see the chapter on discipline for why lamping your children is just plain WRONG).

Surely, surely they'll be sleeping through the night by then? In many cases, unfortunately not. In this chapter we look at:

- How can we encourage our toddlers to sleep through the night?
- What kind of bedtime routine will help our children settle down (relatively) calmly for the night?
- What time should a toddler go to bed?
- How to deal with early morning waking;
- Coping with night terrors;
- How parents of toddlers cope with sleep deprivation;
- When's the best time to move from cot to bed?

You may be one of those parents whose baby slept through the night from an early age and continues to do so now; in which case you can skip this chapter. And by the way, we hate you. We hate your rosy skin, well-rested demeanour and air of contentment. The rest of us are frazzled to within an inch of our lives.

The toughest part about a non-sleeping toddler is that it has gone on for so flipping long that the waking habit may be well ingrained, and you, the parent, may have had about as much as you can take. Often dealing with children's sleep problems requires the adult to stay quite calm and not get wound up, but that's easier said than done when you are exhausted.

I wish someone had told me that sleepless nights will end soon
Take heart from this fact – the end is in sight. Your child has got many more good nights' sleep ahead of them than bad. If you can

grit your teeth and get through this bit then it won't be long before your little threenager becomes a little more teenage and starts sleeping longer than you do.

In fact, they may start to sleep through whilst you're still waking up, as your sleeping patterns have probably changed as a result of years of disturbed nights. They give, and then they take away. If they weren't so adorable the rest of the time they'd never get away with it.

So if you are ground down by a child who refuses to believe in the benefits of a solid 12 hours of rest – above all, take care of yourself. Eat as well as you can, doze during children's telly hours and make sure your partner does their share.

Bedtime basics

Lynda Hudson is a clinical hypnotherapist who specialises in children's problems. Lynda says: 'I think that in general children definitely benefit from routine but that parents also need to have a certain amount of flexibility and be prepared to adapt as and when appropriate.' This is Lynda's advice for calm bedtimes:

How can I get my toddler to calm down before bedtime?
- Plan in plenty of physically energetic activities earlier on in the daytime to use up energy;
- Do clearing up activities earlier on so there are not last minute tantrums because they are over excited / overtired / grumpy at the time when they should be calming down;
- Start calming down activities at least an hour before bedtime e.g. reading;
- Get into a nightly routine which suits your situation as far as possible e.g. early tea time, bath time and gentle story time afterwards followed by bed so that they come to expect, both consciously and unconsciously, to be calming down at that time;

- If relevant, talk with your husband / wife / partner and explain tactfully that boisterous games when they return from work over-excite your child, making bedtime more difficult. Encourage 'quiet time activities' instead;
- Spend quiet time yourself with your child and give him or her as far as possible your undivided attention in this pre-bedtime hour. Since all children crave love and attention they are being unconsciously 'rewarded' by engaging in calming time activities. Talk to them, ask them or remind them about nice things that they did during the day;
- Tell them stories about themselves. They can be based on facts e.g. what they did when they were teeny, tiny babies and how much you loved them. They can be more imaginative about going on a magic carpet and flying off to their favourite place. If you find it hard to be imaginative, base it on a story in a book but change the names to those of your child and siblings or friends;
- Give an older toddler a relaxing, calming and comforting CD to listen to before or around bedtime.

Lynda Hudson
Clinical hypnotherapist
www.firstwayforward.com

Bedtime routine

Regardless of whether you're a stickler for daily routine or more of a go with the flow type, it will be very beneficial to your child if you can establish a bedtime routine that is the same every night. Even if it's the only routine in your day, it's an important one.

What you include is up to you, but a typical toddler's bedtime routine starting 1–2 hours before bedtime and could be based upon on the following pattern:

1. Noisy, energetic play to blow off steam;
2. Bath time – calming, soothing and cleaning – you're never too young to multitask;
3. Ablutions – brush teeth, change nappy or visit the loo. Let your child choose what pyjamas to wear, since this will help them feel more in control of the process and less like they're being dragged towards an unwanted destination;
4. Quiet playing time in the child's bedroom. Watch out for your child getting too hyped up. I have on occasion had to yell 'The reason why it's called Quiet Playing is because you're supposed to be quiet!' thus proving that I'm no better than them when it comes to noise making. But anyway – quiet playing, that's the theory;
5. Bedtime story – many children like the security of a fixed routine and will enjoy the same story every night. Parents may not enjoy this quite so much, so make sure you pick a good one when you start;
6. Thank you and goodnight – let your child choose which toy to cuddle up to and whether they want a dim light on. Again, this helps the reluctant sleeper to feel more in control of what's happening. Music or story tapes can work well at this time. Very fidgety children who find it hard to switch off can often be persuaded to stay in bed if they've got a small toy to hold and a story to listen to – it helps if these are reserved for bedtime only.

How much sleep do toddlers need?
Some children are real night owls and their parents are happy for them to stay up later. If you don't have to be anywhere in a hurry the next day and can compensate with day time naps then this is do-able.

You will know if your child is getting enough sleep depending on how much energy they have the rest of the time. Every child is different, but as a broad guide, the UK National Health Service recommends:

- For two year olds – 11.75 hours of sleep at night, and around 1.25 hours during the day, making a total of 13 hours in any 24 hour period;
- For four year olds – sleep reduces slightly as children get older, and children of this age are recommended to have around 11.5 hours of sleep each night.

So think about what time you want your child to get up in the morning, how much sleep they need, and work out an appropriate bedtime from there. If a child is consistently getting less sleep than they need, then this will negatively affect their development.

If you're trying to move your child from a later to an earlier bedtime, do it in stages. So if bedtime is currently around 10pm, aim for 9.30pm and make it half an hour earlier each week until you get to the bedtime you want your child to have.

What worked for us – Dealing with ongoing lack of sleep
Of course many children do not do things by the book. *Ramblings of a Suburban Mummy* writes at realsuburbanmummy.com about her seemingly endless struggles to get her son to sleep through the night:
'From the minute he was born we have struggled with getting C to sleep at night. Sleepless nights do not a happy mummy make.

'He carried on having a feed in the night for a long time. Everyone told me he didn't need it but I was so tired by this point from the ongoing lack of sleep that I just couldn't face withdrawing the one thing that made him go back to sleep. It's amazing how quickly I give in when I'm tired!

'We got into the horrid position of having C in our bed at some point every night, well it was either that or me on the floor in his bedroom! So we would spend the early hours being kicked, punched, jumped on etc. I was back at work too by this point and it was awful having to get up and go to work after rubbish sleep. I'd catch myself napping on my lunch break just to catch up a little bit, setting the timer on my phone so I didn't sleep too long! Not exactly the best way to deal with it but the only way I could cope.

'Some nights he did sleep through, those nights were absolute bliss. I think those nights are the only thing that kept me going at times, those and the nights he spent at Grandma's house!

'C's sleeping didn't get much better but by the time I was about 28 weeks pregnant I had had enough. I couldn't have C in our bed, I was in too much pain to have him kicking me so I decided to just go in his room and put him back to bed, no fuss, no kisses, just straight back into bed. It nearly killed me! Physically, it was so hard, I could barely walk by this point and grabbing an active toddler was excruciating but so necessary. It took me about 10 days before I could get him to go straight back down in his own bed, but it eventually worked.'
Realsuburbanmummy.com

Disrupted sleep is an ongoing issue for many parents of toddlers, with no single, failsafe solution – but somehow, we find a way through.

I wish someone had told me that not all cries are the same
'When the little blighters can stand in their cot and refuse to lie down, let alone go to sleep, what helped me was to be able to distinguish between their angry cry and their upset cry.

'It's amazing how much more determined you can be when you realise you are dealing with an angry toddler, as opposed to an upset one.

'Now this has to be tackled when you know they are tired (no late afternoon nap etc) and when you have the time, energy and patience. The tip is this – basically just to keep lying them back down, telling them gently it's time to sleep.

'I never walked away – some people do, but I never have or would and I think it helps to stay by the cot side. The first night I attempted this with baby Aiden, I laid him back down 36 times, never left him cry, picked him up and gave him a bit of a cuddle even, but was fair and determined and exhaustion got the better of him eventually.

'The next night it took 19 goes, the following one took 6 and I never had to do it again. There was no controlled crying, no real upset, just plain anger on his part. It wasn't painful for either of us because I didn't leave him and the message was very clear. It was done lovingly throughout and worked!'

Anya Harris
Older Single Mum, oldersinglemum.blogspot.com

Controlled crying

Controlled crying is one of those topics that tends to divide parents. It's not a nice sleep training technique to use, since it involves not responding to your child's cries, which pretty much goes against every parenting instinct you've got. Don't be surprised if it reduces you to tears as well.

There has been criticism of this method, but as far as I can see this has developed from studies where the child was left to cry for much longer periods than you're supposed to stick to when you follow this routine.

Despite the controversy, you can see why parents tend to use this method as a last resort – it works, and when you're on your knees through lack of sleep, you'll try anything.

Controlled crying involves not going in to your baby when they first wake up. The point of doing this is so that your child can learn to settle themselves down again and get back to sleep easily. It's generally not recommended before a baby is aged 6-8 months, but can be used after that. I did it with both my children when they were around two and still waking up at night and it was horrible, horrible, horrible. But it worked, and the switch to a full night's sleep did us all an enormous amount of good.

How controlled crying works

Follow your regular bedtime routine and put your child to bed, then leave the room. When your child wakes up, start by leaving it for two minutes before you go in. The next time, leave it for four minutes, and build up from there in two-minute increments. Repeat as necessary each time your child wakes up. Crucially, this method doesn't mean leaving your child to cry for hours on end.

If you decide to go for controlled crying, the things you need to bear in mind are:

- Parents need to be 100% committed It's not fair on your toddler to do it for a night or two, or even an hour or two, then change your minds;
- Recognise that it will be tough for you. Even if you only leave your baby to cry for two minutes, they'll be the longest two minutes of your life. Only choose to do this when there are no other major stresses and strains happening in your life;
- It helps to tell others. I went and explained to the neighbours that it was going to be noisy for a few nights. Everyone was hugely sympathetic and most said they'd done it too. It also helped my commitment to the process to say it out loud to another person.

Most people find that controlled crying works fairly quickly. So whilst you might have some hideous nights, hopefully there won't be too many. Once you start, you must stick to it, even if things seem to be getting worse before they get better.

What worked for us – Sleep training
'Once Logan reached almost 13 months old I felt it was time to give up the breastfeeding and so I began to gradu-

ally wean him off. With this came the challenge of getting him to sleep through the night. I was very nervous about this and sort of panicked as I thought what would I do to get Logan to sleep as I couldn't comfort him with breast-feeding anymore!

'So it was decided we would use controlled crying as lots of people recommended it and it had the quickest results. We were also very aware that it would be hard to sit there and listen to your baby cry and it definitely was!

'For the first few nights it was really, really hard and sometimes I felt close to tears but we stuck with it. After a week it actually began to work, we were very surprised! In fact it went so well Logan actually got used to going to bed and would happily go to bed without a fuss and sleep from 6.30/7pm to 8 in the morning. So after a year of sleepless nights we were finally rewarded with a happy, sleeping baby.

'I did find it all very exhausting and sometimes I felt like I couldn't be bothered any more but I just had to get on with it and do what was best for my baby.'

Laura Nelson

www.thebreastestnews.co.uk

Other sleep strategies to try
- Calmly take your child back to bed every time they wake up, no matter how many times it takes. Don't engage with them or make a big drama of it and speak very little – be clear that there will be no reward of attention for getting up at night;
- Aim to reintroduce a nap after lunch. Has your child dropped their nap too soon? This could be the reason for disturbed nights;
- Take your child in to sleep with you – this works well for some families with big beds, though many parents find that their toddler seems a little too fond of the midnight karate kicks for this to be a comfortable option.

What worked for us – Night time cuddles
Janice Thompson has one son and has had to deal with disrupted sleep and early morning waking:
'On the whole our little lad is not a bad sleeper. His normal routine is up about 7am and back in to bed for roughly 8pm with approximately a two hour sleep just after lunch.

'That particular routine seems to work best for him and for us, and we really needed to find something that works especially as I'm now back at work.

'We don't tend to run to his room at every whimper (bad parent I know). We usually wait for a few minutes to see if he'll self-settle because we know that if we do go in we'll never get out in under 45 minutes, and especially when it's 3am you really want to get him back to sleep asap!

'What we found works best at 3am is for us to sit and cuddle him in the dark, whilst we watch the ceiling projections from his Tomy DreamStar and listen to its lullabies, it's a fantastic product.

'Once he's calmed down we'll either try him with some milk or some "magic gel" (Bonjela) or even both! After a while we'll try and put him back in to his cot but more often than not it's not very successful on the first attempt, or even the second. Unfortunately it usually means that we then have to start with the calming routine again. Singing always helps at every stage.

'Usually on around the third or fourth attempt we can get him back in to his cot, lots of quiet singing and gentle back rubs when he's in. Eventually once he's calm and almost asleep we can start to retreat backwards out of his room, but again this can take a good few attempts.

'Finally at that point we creep back to our bedroom and flop in to bed, only to be woken a few hours later by the alarm clock!

'I can cope with reduced sleep but when it's night after night it does take its toll and that usually manifests itself around 3pm at work. Strong coffee tends to do the trick at that point.'
Janice Thompson
aworkingmum.com

A calming exercise for toddlers
Marneta Viegas of *Relax Kids* is an expert in getting children to relax and be calmer. And yes you can start with toddlers. She recommends this simple way to introduce meditation and relaxation to older toddlers (around 3 or 4) just before bedtime:

'Wiggle your right foot. Relax the big toe, and all the other toes.
Say goodnight right foot.
Wiggle your left foot. Relax the big toe, and all the other toes.
Say goodnight left foot.
Wiggle your right leg and relax it and say goodnight right leg.
Wiggle your left leg and relax it and say goodnight left leg.
Wiggle your back and relax it and say goodnight back.
Shake your shoulders and stop and relax them. Say goodnight shoulders.
Nod your head and shake your head. Stop and relax your head.
Open your eyes wide and now close them. Open your mouth wide and yawn and now close it.
Say goodnight head.
Goodnight ears, goodnight mouth, goodnight nose, good-night eyes.
Breathe in and breathe out and relax and feel your whole body going to sleep.'
Marneta Viegas
www.relaxkids.com

Dropping the day time nap

Your toddler's daytime and night time sleep are connected. And one factor which will help with sleep as your child gets older is dropping their afternoon nap. All children's sleep patterns are different – some children never really have a big sleep during the day, whilst others can't get through the day without a nap until they are practically at school.

But broadly speaking, most toddlers do cut back substantially on the amount of sleep they need during the day from around two to three. And once they've dropped the nap, even if they're not sleeping, they'll still benefit from some quiet time during the afternoon. This could involve resting on their bed looking at a picture book or snuggling up on the sofa watching a DVD.

Dummy or not?

If your child isn't already using a dummy or soother by the time they hit the toddler stage, then I wouldn't bother with trying to introduce one now. In fact, by this stage you may be more concerned with how to get rid of the dummy.

I wish someone had told me that parents need to give up dummies too

The first thing to be aware of is that you as the parent need to be ready to give up on the dummy before you expect your child to. As parents of dummy users (and yes, both of my children had one) we do get reliant on them to soothe a fractious crier. So when you decide that it's 'bye bye dum dums', make sure that you're mentally prepared to say 'no' or find other alternatives for at least a few days. If you're already exhausted or stressed out about other issues, leave it until those things pass.

How to break the dummy habit completely:

You will make it easier on both of you if you decide to drop the dummy either when your baby is very small, so they forget about it quickly, or when they're old enough to understand that it's time to give it up and talk about it (around 2 or 3). In between these stages is probably the hardest time, because they'll be old enough to make an attachment to their dummy, but not old enough to understand why you want to take it away. Start breaking your (and your child's) dummy habit by stopping taking one out with you during the day.

- Appeal to their sense of maturity. Some children love to be 'the big boy' or 'the big girl', so appeal to them on this level. Point out that they won't want something that marks them out as a baby;
- A visit from The Dummy Fairy. This is the Tooth Fairy's cousin, who leaves gifts for children who give her their dummies;
- Send it to Father Christmas. Did you know that Father Christmas collects up dummies to distribute to all the babies around the world? And then leaves a special gift in return? You do now. The advantage of this technique is that the child is likely to be distracted by the excitement of Christmas;
- Old fashioned bribery. Lacking in imagination, this is what I did. But it is a classic motivational technique – make change more attractive than staying the same. When my child spotted something she liked in a toy shop, I'd say 'You can have that in exchange for your dummies'. Eventually she caved in when she spotted a particularly unattractive hot water bottle cover that she wanted more than the dummies.

How to cope with early morning waking
Has your child been watching too much Postman Pat and started to hanker after a career as an early riser? Unfortunately for parents, there are many toddlers who, though sleeping through the majority of the night, seem to think that 5.30am is a perfectly reasonable time to start the day. There they are bouncing with energy and raring to go as you stare at them through bloodshot eyes and unkempt hair and plead that you are not really a morning person anyway.

One approach you can take to this is to use very thick curtains or blackout blinds in the summer months if you think that light coming in is what's waking your child up. This may work, though as penance your child may then find another way to torture you.

Musical alarm clocks can also be worth a try, if you get something very visual to show to your child and let them know when the day begins. Children under five are still a little young to fully understand telling the time, but there are clocks available for this age group where something very definite and visual happens at alarm time (e.g. a bunny pops up) and a small number of children will respond to this. The rest will laugh down their sleeves at the fact that they suckered their parents into buying another piece of useless tat, and still bounce on your bed at 5am. But like I said, it's worth a try.

Sometimes there is no real solution to early morning waking other than gritting your teeth and getting through one of the more physically difficult phases of development. It will pass, I promise.

Either that or from around 3 they should be able to work out how to turn the telly on themselves and might let you snooze on a little longer. Some parents will also leave out breakfast cereal so their child can sort themselves out in the morning, but your toddler would need to be fairly advanced to make this a viable option (and also not prone to mischief and mess – not known as qualities that most toddlers have in abundance). If you let your child get up by themselves, you may be rewarded by cereal and paint all over the floor. Not really worth it in the long run.

Toddler teething disrupting night time sleep
Even children who have slept well for months can be subject to the return of night waking when their large back molars start to come through. Often there's a gap between these teeth and others coming through, plus they're at the back of the child's

mouth, so you may not be aware that this is what is disturbing their sleep.

If your child starts waking unexpectedly at night, check in case teeth are the culprit and you need to give some sort of pain relief such as teething powders or infant paracetamol. This sort of pain usually lasts for no more than a week, and then you have the relief of knowing that teething is once and for all behind you.

Night terrors

Night terrors are the name given to what happens when a young child sits bolt upright in bed, screaming their head off in terror. Like a lot of alarming children's behaviour, they're very common, probably happen to most children at least a few times, and are harmless. Whilst they can be very disturbing to witness, waking up like this won't do your child any harm or cause lasting damage.

And also like a lot of children's behaviour, the clue to what causes a night waking like this lies elsewhere in your child's life. Pay particular attention to any TV your child watches before they go to bed, even if it seems quite innocuous. Sometimes it doesn't take a lot for a child's overactive imagination to get working.

What worked for us when dealing with night terrors
Kylie Hodges writes in her blog *Not Even a Bag of Sugar* about her son Joseph who was born at 27 weeks, is now two and has had repeated night terrors:
'When Joseph was about nine months old, he started suffering night terrors. Most of the literature suggests night terrors don't start until much later; however, Joseph has never been one for reading the literature.

'Night terrors are part of a broader sleep condition called "confusional arousal". Somewhere between going from deep sleep to lighter rapid eye movement sleep, something becomes disturbed, and the baby screams and cries, often sitting bolt upright, with their eyes wide open, or sometimes still closed.

'It's distressing. In our case, Joseph is a laid back, happy baby, and never has cried much, only for obvious things, and to see him so upset and inconsolable was so distressing. And I blamed myself. I started looking for answers, reading, and asking friends for their experiences.

'I could not locate any studies about premature babies and night terrors, but from my casual discussions with mothers of premature babies, I have found that it is not uncommon for premature babies to suffer from night terrors, often into the later toddler years.

'Joseph's night time activity wasn't always screaming or crying. Sometimes he would cough and cough, I would go into him and hold him, and he would start to laugh, but he would be asleep. On one occasion I put him on the floor to straighten his bed, and he crawled – at this stage he didn't do this when awake. He got to sitting, and he started playing with a toy that when awake, he couldn't work. It was spooky, and this went on in varying degrees for weeks. I was baffled as prior to this he'd been sleeping through.

'I read widely on this topic and these are my conclusions. I focus on night time sleep but the same rules go for naps as well.

•   Do not wake the child. Don't run in to the room. Stay calm, stay quiet, talk in soothing tones. You can pick the child up, but it is better not to and to sit in the room and wait for it to finish. The child is actually asleep, so is still getting refreshing sleep, and if you wake the child, he/she will become sleep deprived and may make the night terrors worse;

•   Observe what happens in these instances. If they keep continuing, you may find it helpful to keep a diary of what happened during the night time routine, what time the terror or arousal occurred, how long it went for etc;

• Eliminate obvious causes first. Sometimes things like pain (teething) or a cold (post nasal drip – the snot running into the back of the throat) can cause these arousals, so it is worth trying an infant painkiller before bed, or saline nasal spray;

• If after trying this approach for a few weeks it doesn't work and the night terrors continue you can do the following: look at the diary of when these incidents occur, wake the child up half an hour before the usual time of an arousal. Wake the child fully, offer a drink, and then resettle. This can break the cycle, but you need to be consistent and do this for 10 days running;

• If after trying these methods it's still happening, you should consult your doctor. Sometimes night terrors can be caused by sleep apnoea or not getting enough oxygen during the night. If your child has had problems with breathing in the past, or is on oxygen, seek medical advice before trying the above. It could be as simple as enlarged adenoids;

• Night terrors can be genetic. My grandmother was a sufferer, and so am I;

• The most important thing to remember is that this is not distressing for the child. It's distressing for the family, for the person listening to it and I think, especially the parent, because it's our job to keep them safe from harm. But the child is asleep and quite content, even though they sound like they are being chased by the Gruffalo.'
Kylie Hodges
notevena.blogspot.com

Should you take a toddler into your bed?
This is a matter of personal preference. Some parents love snuggling up to their little cuddly bundles. Others find that it's like sharing a bed with a mini octopus on fight night and no one gets any sleep. Or you may have been co-sleeping from the start,

and they've never left. Either way, as long as all of the family is happy about it, it's your choice.

Just a warning for potty trainers though: watch out for nappy-less children in bed. I remember once having a dream about water running down a drainpipe, only to wake up and find that my toddler son was lying next to me and peeing down my leg.

What worked for us – Repetition and early morning TV
'Having twins, we have always had to be strict with sleeping or we'd be totally exhausted. We only bring a child in bed with us as a last resort – we resettle without saying any words and leave the room. This is repeated until the child has settled. I used to be worried that one twin would wake the other as they share a room. But after a night when one of my twins was sick, screamed the place down, we stripped and remade the bed, and the other twin didn't stir, I've worried much less about this! It's a rare occurrence that both twins wake together in the night.

'If one twin wakes early in the morning, I try to scoop them out of the cot without waking their sibling. Sometimes the child that's awake can be persuaded to lie in bed with me and we snooze together, or we both head downstairs and start our day slowly with a bit of early morning TV or a book.'
Heather Young
Mother of twin toddlers, youngandyounger.net

When is the best time to move from cot to bed?
Some young children get very attached to their cots and don't want to move out of them. But for safety reasons you will need to, as a child attempting to climb out of a cot is a safety hazard in itself.

For the first few nights that your toddler is in a big bed, put some cushions on the floor in case they fall out. Though really, it's surprising how little this happens. What you might find is more likely to happen is that your toddler takes the opportunity, now they're free from the constraints of the cot, to go wandering around at night.

If this happens, keep it low key and consistent. Calmly take your child straight back to bed – no muss, no fuss. No more stories or songs to be sung. Keep doing this until your child gets the message and realises that you aren't going to be inviting them to stay up and watch a DVD with you.

Take care of yourself
There's plenty of sympathy for the exhaustion experienced by new parents, and rightly so. But for the parents of toddlers? Not so much. And yet it is tough, this long term sleep deprivation – torturers might at least give you time off for good behaviour.

But your child isn't trying to torture you (at least if they are they won't admit to it) – they're just behaving in the only way they know. Learning to sleep through the night is a skill they haven't mastered yet.

Take care of your physical health as much as you can. You may not be in control of how much sleep you get, but you are in control of the rest of your lifestyle – the food you eat, the exercise you take, whether or not you smoke. All of these will have an effect on your energy levels.

Key points about toddlers and sleep
- Use the same bedtime routine every night to get your child calmed down before sleep;
- If your child wakes up, settle them down quickly with very few words;
- This is a good time to get rid of the dummy (though your child may not agree);
- Night terrors are distressing for parents but harmless for children;

- Lack of sleep will affect your child's behaviour and development;
- Controlled crying is tough but effective;
- Early morning waking is very common;
- If your child is a poor sleeper, make taking care of your own health and energy levels a priority.

Why I love my toddlers
'Babies are all very well but all they tend to do is propel things from both ends at inopportune moments, cry, laugh in a gormless fashion and either be asleep or awake at entirely the wrong time.

'For me, children come into their own when they become toddlers. I've always thought it amazing how young kids can be when they develop their own personal likes and dislikes, their own little routines and habits that seem to stay with them for the rest of their life.

'Take Fifi, she's now two and a half and she is IN CHARGE. She chooses her clothes each morning – stripes are very much in at the moment – and tantrums when she doesn't get her very idiosyncratic own way. She's very chatty but not yet at the age where she can tell us why she likes stripes, she just knows that she does and woe betide anyone who thwarts her on that issue.

'Currently Fifi is working on a convoluted bedtime routine that has a set of rules to it but neither my wife or I can fathom them. It involves me carrying her into her bed, being kissed several times, letting her kiss my wife, me tucking her in and then shutting her door. It all has to be done in the prescribed order or there are tears.

'I can also vividly remember when the boy was around that age. He bustled into our room and began piling clothes on our bed. Unsure what the heck he was up to, we let him carry on until he had built a rather wonky pyramid. Apparently he wanted to build a tower all the way

up to the moon. Such is toddler logic, and I wouldn't swap
it for anything else in the world.'
Alex Walsh
Father of two (soon to be three), daddacool.co.uk

Chapter 3: Toddlers at play

Unless you've found a way to power up the laptop from the heat of your child's tantrums, or pimped them out as a child model, play will most likely be the major waking occupation of your under five. Play is a child's work – it's one of the main ways they explore and learn about the world. But what should be fun can also be the source of angst, as children learn to share and not take a chunk out of their friends. In this chapter we're looking at:

- An explanation of common play patterns amongst children of this age, so parents can understand why they play the way they do;
- Co-operative play, and how to encourage sharing;
- Simple ideas for imaginative play;
- The educational benefits of play;
- How do deal with biting during play.

Does a toddler need playmates?
Once your child gets beyond twelve months old, you may find that they're very interested in other children. Everything they do is fascinating. But that doesn't necessarily mean that your growing baby wants to play with others – in fact co-operative playing can take quite some time to develop.

At first, your child may be happy to observe other children (and adults). As they discover their hands and mouth and become more mobile, it may look as though they're getting ready to join in. One thing that your child will love is if you get down on the floor and play at their level – as mentioned in the chapter on behaviour, putting yourself on the same physical level as your child is great for communication.

Now, some readers may be raising their eyes at this point and thinking, 'Blimey, surely nobody needs to be told to play with their child' but in fact, some people do need encouragement with this. Playing with a small child doesn't come naturally to every-body – some parents find it boring and a bit futile, since their interests and their child's probably don't tally. If you still think of yourself as relatively young and together, pointing at buses for 45 minutes simply may not rock your boat. But give it a go and let your child take the lead – it's worth it. If things have been a bit fraught at home and your toddler's been playing up a lot, make a point of playing together more to re-establish your relationship and ensure that your communication isn't all about shouting and saying 'No'.

What worked for us – Physical play
'My toddler is lucky to have two big brothers to play with (aged 9 and 11). Consequently, he plays a lot of chasing and tickling games with them. He loves bouncing on the trampoline, especially if there are bigger children there with him. He enjoys drawing and painting (walls a speciali-ty). One of his favourite toys is a pretend kitchen in which he cooks for ages. Currently he's at the "posting" stage so he spends a lot of time putting things into other things – like keys in the fridge drawer and toast in your handbag. Football is popular, especially when he can find a bigger kid to play with. He will also spend quieter play time on construction toys such as Duplo.'
Ellen Arnison
bundance.blogspot.com

The educational benefits of play
The roots of later learning can be found in even the simplest of games. Teresa Bliss is a Child and Educational Psychologist and recommends that you look for opportunities to learn through play:
'The sorts of things that parents can be doing preschool to help the children's language and listening skills in-clude: using fun activities and books to explore with

children the sounds different animals make, experimenting with different sounds common objects make such as wooden spoons and saucepans.

'The very best thing that parents can be doing with their children is talking to them, teaching them nursery rhymes, teaching them poems with rhythm and teaching them clapping games.

'Give children as many opportunities as possible to experience the world for themselves. For example, take them out to farms, talk to them about what they're seeing, ask them questions and encourage them to ask you questions. Help children to listen to and remember sounds, talk to them about what they can remember they've heard – help them to discriminate between sounds.

'Take children to the local library and help them to develop an excitement and anticipation about books. Encourage them to cook with you, talk to them about what they're doing and let them estimate and measure. This is good for maths and developing the language of maths.

'Find incidental counting opportunities, for example how many footsteps to get upstairs, or from their bedroom to their parents' bedroom? Let them help using the egg timer for cooking eggs and doing other activities. These things may seem rather mundane but developing your child's capacity for listening and responding, developing their language and vocabulary are key skills to equip them for education at school.'

Teresa Bliss

Teresabliss.com

Confident play is easy play

Some parents don't feel particularly confident when it comes to playing with their children. It gets pushed aside because there is always something more important to be doing – it feels almost self indulgent to lose yourself in play. But this is where our children have a lot to teach us – we could probably all do with letting our imaginations loose and playing more. And ultimately you don't really need to do a lot other than to be there – follow your child's lead when it comes to play.

What worked for us – Cheap and easy play with under fives:
'1. Place interesting toys and objects just beyond their reach to encourage your child to move more. For pre-walkers, you can attach some bells or ribbons to socks for them to wear when they are on their backs;

2. Encourage children to walk every day. Start small, walk for 5 minutes, turn around and walk home. Gradually build up the length of time you walk for. Take some water to drink and maybe add a picnic in the middle sometimes;

3. Choose to walk whenever you can. You will need to give yourself more time to get places, but you will have time to talk, sing, observe the landscape, or make a photo book of your walk;

4. Put some music on and simply dance. Move, stretch, crouch, bend, clap, march and sing along. Thinking about the beat of different kinds of music will also help children develop their appreciation of maths and language concepts;

5. Have a selection of scarves, bean bags and balls to throw, catch, roll, kick and even juggle;

6. Create obstacle courses using cushions, cardboard boxes, skipping ropes and anything else you have around. Packaging and cardboard boxes are often more interesting to children than the toys they may contain. Make the most of the time when a cardboard box will do – you won't get away with it forever;

7. Find some big spoons and potatoes and have potato and spoon races. Emphasise that in this case "slow and

steady" really does win the race! This will help your child become more patient and build persistence.'
Sarah Cruickshank
Writer, virtual PA, Scout Leader and mother of one
www.sarahcruickshank.co.uk

Small world play

As your toddler grows and becomes better at expressing themselves, they may move on to what's known as small world play. This is literally mimicking the grown up world in miniature – making a small world.

It's fascinating to observe as your child holds a tea party with their teddies or drives cars along the carpet because you will start to get an insight into how they see the world. And if you look at how your child 'parents' their dollies and soft toys, you'll get a reflection of how they see their own parents – and you might not like all you see.

If you are having problems with your child's behaviour, or if there are stresses and strains at home, encourage more small world play and watch how they behave. Your child will probably be more relaxed when they're playing with a world that they're in charge of, which may tell you more about how they're feeling than mere words could.

Construction play

Any type of building play is great for under fives as it helps their understanding of how things fit together, plus it increases hand/eye co-ordination and fine motor skills. You may also find that your child likes to hide things; this is because they're reinforcing their sense of object permanence – the knowledge that things don't disappear when you can't see them. So when your house keys turn up inside a sock, don't be angry with your child – they were just learning and not deliberately trying to send you bat-crazy bonkers. At least in theory, anyway.

Toddlers: an instruction manual

What worked for us – messy play

Cathy James is a mother of two and an outstanding-rated childminder who specialises in working with pre-school children. She's passionate about the value of messy play: 'Messy play is a fantastic fun activity for toddlers, who love exploring the world through their senses, and you can use lots of inexpensive things you have at home for them to play with. If you're worried about too much mess, take some precautions and then you can relax and let the kids enjoy themselves. Cover up yourself, your toddler and the floor, or better still, take the play outside.

'You can use an empty paddling pool in the house and put the messy play inside it, to help contain the play and stop the mess spreading throughout the room.

'The bath is another good location for messy play, as you can just pull the plug and let everything drain away when you've finished. We like to add a few drops of food colouring to the bathwater, to blow bubbles and to add in some ice cubes that have been dyed different colours.

'If you're worried about your child putting everything in their mouth, then let them play with food and it doesn't matter if they do eat a little. Cooked spaghetti, different colours of jelly to mix or boiled potatoes to chop and mash are all lots of fun to play with.

'Toddlers love being just like mum and dad so whenever you can allow a little extra time and let them join in with whatever you're doing. I think we sometimes forget that cooking, sweeping the floor and sorting laundry are a much fun as playing with toys when you are two. Letting your child join in starts to teach them important skills, gives you lots of opportunity to chat and encourage their language development, and of course gives you the chance to get some chores done too.'

Cathy James
NurtureStore, nurturestore.co.uk

What worked for us – imaginative play

Susie Newday is a mother of five who thinks that active and imaginative playtime is in danger of being overlooked: 'My fifth child has spent more hours than I can count playing with plastic cups, shells, coins and dried apricot pits and a mini ceramic tea set. She loves my yoga mat and finds all different uses for it. She loves lining things up, especially in rows. She loves colouring and folding up papers. Like the million paper fans she drew and folded and lined up. (Told you she had an obsession with lining things up.) She can have whole conversations with her dolls (and herself). She has an imagination and makes her own toys. She loves balls. She loves spinning. And of course my little monkey loves monkeys. Playing is hard work.'

Susie Newday

www.newdaynewlesson.com

Parallel play

Parallel play is a term used to describe what happens when children play alongside each other, rather than joining in a game together. It's a very natural play stage for younger toddlers.

Don't be worried if your toddler doesn't seem to join in with others much – they may still be enjoying playing alongside them very much. Co-operative play, where children fully engage with each other in a game, will follow later on. Watch out for clashes if your toddler is playing next to an older child, who may be expecting them to join in the game more than they are able to.

I wish someone had told me that the playful stage gets better every day

Emma's daughter is about to turn two.

'I think she's at a fantastic age because she learns new things on a daily basis. Sometimes it is things you've taught her but other times you have no idea how she's learnt them and it amazes you.

'She's really funny and gets more amusing every day as her imagination grows. She makes us cups of tea with her little tea set, although you must ensure there is a spoon in your cup too, and uses the saucers to give us dinner (which you must eat with two spoons). She gives her teddies tea and dinner, sometimes even her books or ball too.

'There are so many things that she amazes us with on a daily basis and we frequently tell each other how great she is and wonder why can't she stay this big forever. But she continues to grow into a gorgeous, funny, sensitive little girl who makes me so happy and I just wonder; does it just keep getting better?

'I would like to be able to stop time. She's at a great age; chattering away, learning new things daily, beginning to develop a sense of humour, and part of me doesn't want this bit to end. I don't want her to stop talking long enough to watch a film or become self-conscious about singing rhymes at the top of her voice in the supermarket. I want to keep my baby just a little longer.'
www.mummymusings.co.uk

Share and share alike
Sharing is a lifelong skill, which we can start to introduce at the toddler stage, but it's tough. Other people's toys are always more interesting than your own. Even if your child is engaged in parallel play, that doesn't mean that they won't be interested in whatever other toys are around. And when you've got more than one child faced with a variety of toys, problems can arise.

Expecting children to share their toys is a bit of a misnomer, because unless the toy can be physically split in two, what you are really asking is for the child to give their toy to another child, when they may be quite happily playing by themselves. It's understandable that they might not grasp what you mean, and are likely to get upset.

This is where you need to be explicitly clear in the language you use so that your child knows what's expected of them. A really helpful technique is to count to five or ten while your child plays, and explain that it'll be someone else's turn after that. Then count again whilst that child plays and make sure your child gets the toy back again when it's their turn. Children are often much happier to give something up temporarily if they know it's coming back. You can help your child get better at taking turns by practising this technique when you're playing with them.

Watch out for times when your child shares well and give lots of praise and attention for this. Let them know when they get it right and they're more likely to do it again.

When your child won't play nicely

Many toddlers hit and bite. It doesn't mean they're a delinquent in training. It means that they're lacking in control, feeling frustrated and generally acting like a classic toddler. And it probably means that they're after more of your attention.

Make sure your child gets as much physical exercise and running around time as possible – this gives a safe space to work out physical frustrations. Look out for times when your child is behaving well and give lots of praise and occasionally a little sticker as a reward. If you know that your child has a tendency to hit or bite then you owe it to yourself and them to be extra vigilant when they're around other children. And think ahead before you get into social situations – is your child likely to be tired, hungry or bored? Any of these can affect their behaviour.

If a child is having problems socialising then the answer is not to socialise less – if anything they would probably benefit from more time amongst their peer group. Watch out for how your child behaves in different settings – perhaps they will be more comfortable with playing in a small gathering rather than a noisy toddler playgroup.

Use a technique that works for you to address this. The 'naughty step' is very popular these days, but that doesn't mean that it works for every child. Another method which can be very effective is counting to three and letting your child know that they will be punished if they don't do as you ask before you get to three.

Only threaten a punishment if you intend to carry through with it – children are very adept at recognising empty threats. Get down on your child's level and look them in the eye when you speak to them. You don't need to shout, but you do need to be firm.

Also, focus on what you want your child to do, rather than what you don't want them to do – this draws attention to the behaviour you want, rather than what you don't want. If you say no less often, then your child will be more inclined to take notice when you do say it. So rather than talking about the hitting, talk about the kind of behaviour you want to encourage – smiling, gentleness, kind hands and so on.

Toys in the mouth
Children up to around age three will still mouth the toys they play with – they're interested in the world from every angle, so using their mouths to explore how something feels and tastes is just part of the game for them. Continue to be vigilant for small objects which your child could put in their mouth. This can be an added stress for parents as you become always on alert for potential choking hazards.

It's amazing how parents of toddlers quickly develop skills that take police officers years to learn. We can scan a room in seconds and judge where dangers lurk. It's a bore, but something you need to do. And you will develop the innate ability to do this, and surprise yourself by spotting a pair of scissors on a low lying shelf within two seconds of entering the room.

How to deal with biting

The not so nice end of toddlers' compulsion to explore things with their mouths is that some can and do bite other children. If your child is a biter, you'll need to be extra vigilant when you're both around other children who may not appreciated being chomped on. Little children who bite don't tend to do it out of nastiness or a desire to cause pain – it's more a case of lack of impulse control, and a failure to grasp the fact that you don't bite your mates.

In situations like this, it becomes all the more important that you're not constantly telling your child 'No!' – limit how often you say it, and a short sharp 'No!' will have an immediate effect. If you are constantly saying 'No' to your child then it won't be as effective as it would be if you did it less often. But when a child bites, you need to get the message across quickly – with your words, behaviour and body language – that this is not acceptable behaviour.

Give your attention to the child who's been bitten rather than the one who's doing the biting. Little children's behaviour is essentially designed to draw your attention (whether positive or negative attention, they don't really mind as long as your focus is on them), and so they'll soon get the message that biting doesn't work in this respect.

Distract your child with something else – perhaps a toy or something to chew on. It could very well be that their gums are genuinely sore and they need something cool to chew, like a cold carrot or a teething ring. Anything other than their best pal from nursery.

Don't bite them back

There used to be a school of thought that the best way to deal with a biter was to bite them back, but this is outmoded now and frankly pretty mean. If you resort to tactics like this then you've most definitely lost control of the situation and probably need a bit of Time Out yourself.

What message would you be sending if you bit them back? 'Hey, biting's so much fun, mummy's joining in!', or, 'Be scared of Dad, he can bite harder than you!'

Parenting has moved on and so have you. Biting them back is not the answer. If your child is a biter, it's a very common phase, and not necessarily anything you're doing wrong as a parent. But if you start to bite them back, it will be.

When it comes to play, your child's the expert
As Tim Atkinson found, the key to play is letting your child take the lead:

The Wheels on the Bus
A PLAY WOT I WROTE
In One Act
By Me.

Cast:
A helper
A stay-at-home dad
Charlie, a three-year-old stickler for detail

Scene:
Toddler group singalong

Helper:
Right children, what shall we sing first today? Any suggestions?

Charlie:
I'd like to sing 'The Wheels on the Bus' please.

Helper:
The Wheels on the Bus? Of course, Charlie. Now, let's all do the actions.

(The group sings.)
The wheels on the bus go round and round,
round and round, round and round,
The wheels on the bus go...'

Charlie *(interrupting)*:
Excuse me...

Helper:
What is it Charlie?

Charlie:
Well, the wheels on the bus go round like this. *(Mimes action of wheels turning.)* You were doing the actions to the wheels on the train.

Helper:
I was?

Charlie:
Yes you were. The wheels on the train go round like this. *(Mimes action of pistons turning.)* You were doing the wheels on the train.

Helper:
Oh well I'm very sorry Charlie. Shall we start again?

All:
The wheels on the bus (etc.)

(Later...)
...The babies on the bus go wah wah wah
wah wah wah, wah wah wah...

Dad: *(whispering)*

Charlie, why are you still doing the action for the wheels on the bus? We've done the wipers on the bus, and the mummies on the bus; now we're doing the babies.

Charlie:
Yes, I know daddy.
But if someone doesn't keep the wheels turning the bus will stop moving and we won't be able to sing anything.

Dad:
Ah...

THE END.

Tim Atkinson
Bringing Up Charlie, bringingupcharlie.co.uk

Key points about toddlers and play:
• Play is an essential part of a toddler's social and educational development;
• Encourage as much imaginative play as you can – and join in as much as possible;
• Don't worry if you child doesn't want to play with others just yet;
• Give attention for positive behavior;
• Biting is fairly common – give attention to the victim and a short, sharp 'No' to the biter;
• Enjoy this playful stage while it lasts.

Why I Love My Playful Toddler
'There was once a small person who just kind of laid on the floor and made gurgling noises and kicked her legs a bit, who over time has become a proper little lady; who can say "oh my goodness" now instead of "oh my god" (phew), will say "I love you mummy! (or daddy)" and

gives endless cuddles and songs and love – and all you need to give her are endless love, songs and cuddles back (as well as a spot of parenting thrown in for good measure).

'This little person copies, absorbs, repeats days later and keeps going. You can tell her what you'd like to do, some of the time she might not want to, but if you can suggest reasons why it's good she does it, she appears to understand and will do it (eventually). She'll have her angry moments (don't we all?) but those pass, and the more she communicates why she's angry or upset, the more it feels like we're progressing.

'I love when she'll talk about something which has nothing to do with anything at all, randomly sitting at the table telling us about a squirrel she saw in the back garden three months ago, or how all the people she knows are "pink" ("but daddy is red"), the randomness of her telling us "We'll go to the park tomorrow" (who's the boss here?) but then follow it with a big cuddle and a huge belly laugh giggle. What's not to love?'

Jo Brooks

Holly Blog, misshollyblog.blogspot.com

Chapter 4: Food and fussy eaters

If you've got a faddy eater on your hands, at least you're not alone. When toddlerdom strikes and children learn to say no, fussy eating is at its height. Your compliant little baby who opened their mouth obediently like a bird when offered milk or mushed up food may one day morph into the toddler who clamps their mouth shut and refuses to try anything that's not immediately recognisable. So in this chapter we'll be looking at:

- What causes fussy eating?
- What's the best way to deal with food refusers and ensure they get the nutrition they need?
- How can you encourage your child to be more open to trying new foods?
- How much food should a child of this age be eating?

We will also be scraping a lot of fish fingers into the bin.

I wish someone had told me it wasn't my fault
There's no real rhyme or reason as to why some children get fussier about food than others, and it certainly doesn't make you a bad parent if you find you have a food avoider on your hands.

Neither does it make you a better parent if your child is an omnivore who's always happy to try new things. Two children brought up in the same household by the same parents could have entirely different approaches to food.

That said, if, deep down, you know that your own approach to food and trying new things is less than positive, then don't be surprised if your child picks up on this. And if that's the case, then the place to start making improvements is within your own attitudes rather than your child's. Be honest – does your child see you eating a varied, balanced diet? Are you up for new food experiences, even if it's something you don't expect to like? Does all the family regularly share meals together?

Our survey says...

A survey (conducted by MyVoucherCodes.co.uk in April 2011) of nearly 1,200 UK parents found that almost half of under fours are picky about food.

According to the study, 42% of the parents asked admitted that their children were 'fussy eaters'. However, just under a third (31%) of the parents polled stated that their children will eat 'any food' that they give to them. The remaining 27% said that their child was 'occasionally' a fussy eater. So these results would indicate that it is far more common to have a toddler who refuses at least some food, than it is to have a child who'll eat anything.

The respondents who admitted that their children were 'fussy eaters' were asked to select from multiple answers what foods their children regularly refused to eat. The top ten results were as follows:

1. Cauliflower – 68%
2. Cabbage – 64%
3. Sprouts – 61%
4. Minced beef – 57%
5. Onions – 54%
6. Rice – 52%
7. Cheese – 48%
8. Carrots – 43%
9. Eggs – 41%
10. Peas – 39%

To be fair, I don't think I'd be leaping for joy if I was presented with much of that list. Are there really children who enjoy their sprouts and ask for more? I've yet to meet one.

The parents who admitted that their children were fussy eaters were subsequently asked if they 'encourage' their children to eat the foods that they claim to dislike, to which more than a third, 34%, answered 'no'. When asked to explain their reasons for not encouraging their children to do so, 48%, said it was because of the 'tantrums' thrown by their child, when they try to persuade them to eat foods that they dislike. So could this be why fussy eating seems so widespread?

If your child is prone to tantrums when faced with food they don't like, don't use that as an excuse to give in to them. You'll be sending the message that tantrums get you what you want – and that is a dangerous message for any toddler. It'll probably encourage them to tantrum more, not less, so tread carefully.

What worked for us – One new food at a time
'I introduced one new food at a time, and served it with current favourites. They are more likely to try one new food in amongst others they recognise than introducing a whole plateful of new colours and textures at one time. You can also do this by feeding them the new food from your plate rather than putting it on their own plate.

'I fed Child No1 with chicken soup and a slice of wholemeal bread for breakfast for approximately three weeks at one stage. She asked for it and she ate it, who says breakfast must be cereals?

'Child No3 was notorious for not wanting to eat a meal at what I considered meal times, so he was served finger foods, a selection of which was placed in a plastic box on the table at meals times and he ate when he was hungry. The rule was he had to sit at the table and eat, no wandering around with food was allowed. If there were any of meal 1 remaining then it was thrown away when meal 2 was placed in a fresh box. He did not get treats or sweets if there was food in the box when we went out.'
Elaine, mother of 5 and grandmother of 2
fun-as-a-gran.blogspot.com

I spy something beginning with pea!
My son used to come to the door of the kitchen and scream in horror if he spotted that there was something new on his plate. It didn't even have to be something he actively disliked – if he hadn't encountered it before, then that was enough to set him off.

All you can do with tantrums like this is ignore, ignore, ignore. Eventually (and you may be in for a long wait) they will stop. The first day my son sat next to his plate and asked about the food rather than hollering in horror, I felt like doing a victory dance. Of course, he still didn't eat the ruddy stuff, but at least it was a start.

Only a fifth of the total respondents in the survey previously mentioned said that they were 'persistent' with asking their children to try foods that they claimed to dislike the first time they ate it. In contrast, more than a quarter, 26%, cited that they 'rarely' tried to convince their children to try foods they had previously claimed to dislike. When the respondents who admitted to 'rarely' encouraging their children to try foods more than once were asked why this is the case, 37% said it was because it was 'easier' to just give their children the foods that they liked. And although we might judge the parents who do this (even though we've probably done it ourselves), we can understand it.

What worked for us – Praise and vegetables
'My son went through a really fussy stage with eating. He wouldn't get past the tentative licking of a lot of foods. Tiring of making meals only for them to be wasted, I came up with a plan.

'We spent the next week eating at the table with him and giving him completely over-the-top praise every time he ate something. I really wanted to concentrate on getting him eating veg like broccoli and cauliflower so we had them with every meal that week. In a few days he could say the word 'broccoli' and was munching

away. He still asks for it now and tries everything we put in front of him – he even eats raw onion!'
Kate, mother of two
Life, Love and Living With Boys, lifeloveandlivingwith-boys.wordpress.com

Why do toddlers refuse food?
The calorie needs of a toddler are very different to that of a baby. If you think about how much a baby grows in the first year of its life, from freshly hatched newborn to strong and sturdy nearly-toddler, you can see that it is inevitably going to take a lot of fuel to make that happen. But their rate of growth then slows down and is less consistent from around 12 months onwards. On the other hand, a toddler is much more mobile than a baby and is going to need to power all that fizziness and moving about.

So you may find that your child's appetite goes in fits and spurts just like their growth and activity pattern. Some under fives seem to go for days existing on only fresh air and dried up crisps off the floor, then launch into three course meals with abandon.

Don't panic if it looks like your toddler isn't eating much. Look at the overall picture to get a sense of whether your child is getting the nutrition they need:
• Do they have enough energy for play?
• Do they sleep well, or at least as well as they ever have? If they wake up in the night, are they hungry?
• Does their skin look healthy and bright?
• Are their bowel movements regular and normal (no loose stools or constipation)?
• Are they prone to illness?
A toddler's appetite may also be affected by teething – a sore, gummy mouth would put anyone off their dinner.

Expert Opinion
Author Hollie Smith's nine parenting books include *Dealing With Difficult Eaters*. Hollie says:

'The main advice I have for parents who are worried about their fussy eater is: don't worry. I appreciate this is a tip to be filed under advice that's "easier said than done", but the truth is, your best bet is not to fret. Yes, it's natural to be concerned if your toddler is refusing so many sorts of food it's a wonder he's still able to function. But showing you care is the worst thing you can do.

'Most fussy eating toddlers behave the way they do because they're pushing boundaries. They have little control over any aspect of their lives, except at the dining table, where they've noticed they have power to provoke a reaction. So, psychologically speaking, you need to convince them you don't care. It's hard, really hard, when you've spent hours in the kitchen trying to make something that will tempt them, only to be scraping it in the bin once it's been rejected, but that's what you need to aim for.

'Look at what your child's eating – not just in the course of a day but over the whole week. You might find it's not such a bleak picture as you think. Of course a balanced diet with lots of different things in it is the ideal, but on the other hand, kids can get by pretty well on a few basics.

'Don't be tempted to let them fill up on total rubbish, however, or you'll quickly end up in a vicious cycle where that's all they will eat. Make sure whatever you offer has some sort of nutritional value. The old cliché, that they will eat when they're hungry, can usually be drawn on here.

'If you're truly worried about your child's health because you feel that one or more major food groups are entirely unrepresented in their diet, then by all means take him along to the doctor and get his general health checked out. But be prepared – if your child looks like a reasonably healthy individual with a full complement of energy – for your doctor to send you away again with the same advice: don't worry.'

Don't worry, be happy (and punch a cushion when you need to)

For the parent of a child who seems to hate food, it can be terribly stressful to be faced with this every meal time, several times a day. So, as much as the advice is not to worry, we all know that, as Hollie says, it's easier said than done. And then if you and your partner have different approaches, that can be a cause of stress as well. So talk about it and make sure that your approach is consistent. If parents don't put up a united front, children are quick to play on this.

Your best ally in all of this may be closer than you think, and it's this: other people.

Talk to other people about how you feel. Notice how other children do and don't eat – your child may have a much more adventurous appetite than you realise. Other parents of toddlers are probably tearing their hair out just as much as you are. It's one of those things that goes on behind closed doors, that we don't always talk about. And if you don't know many other parents, go online and find them there.

Though a slight warning: when you do talk to other parents, you may encounter someone who wants to fix you or your child. Ignore them – neither of you are broken. And once you realise that your experience is actually pretty normal, disengage with it. Just walk away. Don't let meal times become a drama.

The toddler's point of view
This is what Hazel Gaynor of *Hot Cross Mum*'s three year old thinks about the matter:

'Ten reasons not to eat your tea
(as compiled by my three and a half year old)

That's too soft, I only like crunchy things.
But that tomato is too bendy.
Well, it's just that those carrots are touching the peas.
Yukky. That bit of the banana is dirty.

I WANTED CHEESE ON TOAST, NOT CHEESE SANDWICHES!

It's just that my tummy is SO full but my pudding tummy is still hungry.

But I can't eat it mummy because THIS IS THE WRONG SPOON!

I'm too tired to eat cucumber.

That's got peppers in it and they make me cough.

But if I eat all this, then I won't have room for any telly.

Is it any wonder that I feel like I am fighting a losing battle?!'

Hazel's woes continue:

'Oh. My. God.

'I don't know if there are enough words in the English language to sufficiently describe how I feel about mealtimes with the children. Despair, exasperation, injustice, futility....

'I sit at the kitchen table, four year old to my right, two year old to my left and feel like I'm about to emerge from the trenches and face a hail of enemy fire. It occasionally starts out quite promisingly. Everyone comes running to the table in anticipation of the latest gastronomic delight and yet within a matter of minutes there is a cacophony of complaining and whingeing and refusing to eat and I want to poke my eyes out with a rusty stick and run for the hills.

'I coax. I cajole. I pep talk. I play trains. I am every Thomas character that has ever been invented going into a tunnel mouth. Twenty minutes pass and we're still working our way through the meal. Then more complaining. Disinterest. Messing with drinks. Anything to distract from the business of eating.

'Thirty, forty minutes may go by as mouthful by painful mouthful we make a little bit of progress. And then I realise I have a fork in each hand, feeding two mouths either side of me and it all seems so ridiculous. I promised myself last week that this would be the last time I physically fed them both. I promised myself the same thing the week before, and the week before that and so on and so on.

'"It's just a phase" my friends tell me and I want to believe they are right. But how long is a phase technically a phase and at what point is it acceptable to throw your hands in the air and the dinners on the floor? (I would not recommend this approach by the way as this just means you have to clean the floor as well as feel crap.)

'So tomorrow I will, again, approach the dinner table with a heavy heart and a forced smile; I will "big-up" the meal as the most delicious thing known to mankind, offer promises of wonderful things to come if everything is eaten up nicely and hope, hope, hope that I emerge on the other side relatively unscathed.'

Hazel Gaynor

Hotcrossmum.blogspot.com

What to do if your child eats very little

First of all, ensure that whatever they do eat is the best possible quality you can get. Yes I know some of that organic, free range stuff is pricey, but at least you are saving on all the stuff they won't eat.

Keep portions very tiny to start with – you can always add more. Look at your child's fist – that's how big their stomach is. It's not a lot of space is it? I know they seem to expand like a snake when it comes to capacity for cake, but for normal meals even what seems like a tiny amount can make a difference.

Praise whatever your child does eat, especially if they've tried something new, but don't turn it into a major fiesta. Calm, disengaged but objectively interested is the attitude we're going for, rather than watching every morsel that passes their lips as if your life depended on it.

What worked for us – Cooking together
'Getting your little ones to help out with the growing and cooking definitely helps! My three year old daughter used to dislike leafy vegetables, until we got her growing her own salad. She has had no problem eating them ever since.

'You can also try the "eating this makes you ..." technique, they seem to love to be taller / bigger / stronger / faster!'
Angela Cheung, mother of two
angela-thisislife.blogspot.com

Remember who's in charge

Sometimes parents moan 'Well, all he'll eat is fish fingers/smiley faces etc', but never forget that this is your choice, not theirs. Your child didn't go down to the supermarket and buy that food with their own money, did they? And if you don't get it in, if it simply isn't in the house to cook, then they may have no choice but to try something else.

Don't engage with it or let mealtimes become a drama (yes I know I said that already, but given that it's easier said than done I'm going to say it twice). In a busy household, being fussy about food may be the only way your child knows to successfully gain your full attention. And this is why stopping drawing attention to it is often key to moving beyond this behaviour. So resist the temptation to try and cajole your child to eat. If my son refuses a meal I just calmly take the plate away, and he usually then wants it back. It was all a game really.

What worked for us – Colour coding
'Kieran went through a fussy eating stage when he was around two and a half years old. He only wanted to eat red foods, which to him meant baked beans, spaghetti in sauce, ravioli etc. We got past this by letting him have one meal a day that was a certain colour. A yellow lunch

was cheese, banana sandwich, etc. Blue day was challenging!'
Nicki Cawood, mother of two
curlyandcandid.co.uk

I wish someone had told me not to give a flying fig about meal times
Helen Redfern found that she was blessed with not one, but two fussy eating toddlers:
'When my son was 21 months old, he wouldn't eat a sodding thing except for the marmite toast I put in front of him. He would refuse homemade chicken and rice casserole (previously a favourite), eggy bread and anything with a tomato tinge.

'My daughter is now 21 months. She is absolutely delightful in so many ways. She's been walking now for a year, is beginning to talk and can say three words together. But, at the moment, she won't eat much. She won't even eat rice pudding which has been my fail safe for so many months. It is toast, or porridge, or fig biscuits, or nothing. Tonight she's had honey on toast. Then I had rice pudding for her. But she refused it after two mouthfuls. And I lost it. I just got so upset. I have homemade banana bread, scones with cream and jam, or the aforementioned pudding and she's just not interested.

'Parents of younger children, take note: do not give your child even the merest hint that you give a flying fig about what they eat. Don't even look at their plate. What seems like a big deal at the time, in fact, isn't. They'll grow out of it. Her teeth will cut and she'll start trying new things. I've seen evidence of that starting with corn on the cob, broccoli and tomato (she never ate them, but she did put them to her lips without spitting in disgust. I call that progress.)

'This anxiousness that I sometimes get in the pit of my stomach may be a little reminder of what has been

before. But it also reminds me that I survived the first time. And I will this time too.'
Helen Redfern
Helenredfern.com

What worked for us – Yummy sounds and dinosaurs
Lisha Aquino Rooney found some novel ways to get her son to try new tastes:
'I laughed when one friend told me to make 'yummy' sounds as I was introducing these new foods to my son. What exactly is a 'yummy' sound? And surely my son can see how incongruous my wannabe scrummy sounds and facial expressions are. 'Tis true that while tasting – and sometimes even smelling – some of his baby food, I gagged.

'While it seemed brilliant advice at the time, the suggestion to use cookie cutters to make different-shaped foods so as to entice my little sweetie to try new grub backfired. Ultimately, he only wanted dinosaur-shaped sandwiches, teddy bear-shaped pancakes and star-shaped papayas. Not easy to accommodate when we're away from home and he refused to eat the food in its usual shape. Using a butter knife, I tried to carve a Diplodocus into a tuna sandwich, and it came out looking like a Tyrannosaurus Rex. He ate the Diplodocus for lunch and then spewed out the bits he didn't want.'
Lisha Aquino Rooney
www.oomphalos.co.uk

I wish someone had told me to chill out more
Tracy Cazaly is a mother of two girls who blogs at *Family, Parents, Girls, Devon*. Her daughters are now past the toddler stage, but she remembers it well:

'My youngest daughter, Jessica, who is now 10 years old, was an incredibly fussy eater and had a very limited eating plan. Now this for me was a whole new experience as my first daughter, Harriet, now 13, ate anything and everything! At first, I found it quite frustrating but very quickly began to realise that like animals she ate when she was hungry. Although, she would only entertain a few foods, if I was happy to give her those which happened to be things like pesto pasta, sausages, bread, tomatoes (which she eats tons of to this day in any form), she would eat a sensible amount. So why beat myself up over it?

'Thankfully, it seemed to have worked and over the past couple of years, Jessica began eating many new things and is actually enjoying the challenges of something new and tasty almost on a daily basis now! What I have found very interesting is that Jessica eats when she is hungry and Harriet eats when she is hungry, emotional, bored and so on... whether there is a link, who knows but I am rather pleased that I took the chilled approach and feel for Jessica it was the right decision.'
Tracy Cazaly
familyparentsgirlsdevon.blogspot.com

Fussy eaters abroad
So say you have the proverbial fussy toddler, and you've chosen to take the path of ignoring their bleatings about the fact that they can't have yoghurt for every meal. This may be OK in the privacy of your own home, amongst your immediate family, but what happens when Grandma comes to stay? Or you're eating out as part of a bigger group?

Well, first of all it might not be as bad as you think. Some children cope better than you might expect with new situations and may be willing to try something new if they can see other people (particularly children) enjoying it. And if your child goes to nursery and is eating away from the home setting (with all its associations) then this can be a chance for them to try something new away from the pressure of home. Peer pressure, even the unconscious kind, can kick in very early, and you may find your child becomes attracted to certain foods simply because they saw them in somebody else's lunchbox.

Toddler lunchboxes

Don't feel that your toddler's nursery lunchbox has to always be full of the old familiars – it could be an opportunity to introduce something new. Here are some tips for putting together a lunchbox for your toddler that stands a chance of getting eaten, from Caroline Job at *Lunchbox World* (Lunchboxworld.com):

1. Make the lunch box look appealing.
If it doesn't look colourful and appetising to you, it most likely won't to them. So they are less likely to tuck in. So think colour – carrots, red pepper, apples, cucumber.

2. Make it easy to eat.
Kids often have just 10–15 minutes for their packed lunch at nursery, before they are encouraged to play outside. So make it easy for them to eat, have things bite size, finger food and watch out for hard to open containers. Compartment lunch boxes can help to keep food separate.

3. Get them to help prepare their own lunch box.
They're more likely to eat their packed lunch if they've helped make it – it'll make them feel more in control of the process.

4. Keep the lunch box and lunch bag smelling fresh.
Smell is such a powerful sense. If the lunch bag starts to smell, it's the first thing they'll notice, even just subconsciously.

5. Keep children hydrated and concentrating hard until the end of the day.

We are like a car and we'd never think of running out of petrol, so our bodies are the same. We also need fuel – water and nutrients to keep those concentration levels up. Nothing worse than picking up a bad tempered child with food rage at home time!

What worked for us – Princess sparkles!
Michelle Hanlon has a great tip, courtesy of her daughter:
'Her eating has got worse and she now doesn't eat much and I find I have to search out ways of making her eat. She likes some foods one day and not another. I now have "princess sparkles" that I "sprinkle" on her food and she eats it. The sparkles are thin air but she sees me go into a cupboard and then she cannot see behind the door.'
Michelle Hanlon
michellehanlon.blogspot.com

It worked for us – Never give up
Wendy is a mother of two who has some amazing recipes on her blog *Mum in Awe* and has found that her children will eat anything – apart from tomatoes.
'I always gave my kids fresh food, and also gave them food I didn't like, and just ate a tiny bit myself. It helped them learn to eat everything and be less fussy than me.

'I did not give them sweets or chocolate, and substituted them for carrots, sugar beans (which they still adore) and sweet apples and fruit. I never included crisps in lunch, or "easy" meals in a packet. Yes, it was hard, but after three years, the kids begin choosing their foods, and by then my kids learnt to choose the healthy option (mostly), so in the long run, I win.

'At times all kids refuse food. I didn't mind as long as they drank liquids, and kept hydrated. If it was a particular food or meal, then the alternative was always fresh fruit. Good or bad, it has turned my kids into fruit lovers, and they generally choose fruit over another less healthy option these days. If my children went on a "two day grape diet", I let it happen. Three days was my limit, then I'd encourage another fruit, or something slightly more substantial. Generally by then they'd be sick of grapes anyway.

'My kids don't like tomatoes. It's the only thing they don't eat. I love tomatoes, but realised at toddler age that the tart acidic taste is what they don't like, so I have never forced them to eat raw tomatoes. They eat tomato paste on pizza or in stews, so I'm not worried about not eating raw tomatoes.

'Why does my kid eat everything? Because they've TRIED everything. You have to make the effort in the early years to reap the benefit in the later years. Before they can say "No" all the time, and before other people teach them unhealthy habits. A few tough years being conscientious results in a lifetime of good habits and healthier adults.'
Muminawe.com

Key points about food and fussiness:
- Your child probably needs a lot less food than you think they do;
- Think in terms of the bigger picture rather than stressing about individual meals;
- Ignore any food refusals and don't fuel fussiness with attention;
- Keep offering new foods, even if you think they'll be refused;
- Although having a fussy eater is undeniably stressful, try not to let it show.

Why I love my toddlers

'Sometimes I forget how small my children are.

'Sometimes I forget that all they really want is a cuddle, a blanket and a favourite teddy.

'Sometimes I forget that I didn't like broccoli either when I was a child.

'Sometimes I forget to be amazed by their smartness, love, cuteness and wonder at the world.

'Sometimes I forget to put that lovely picture they brought home up on the fridge.

'Sometimes I forget to tell them how much I love them and how proud I am of them.

'Sometimes I forget that reading one more chapter of a favourite story is more important than starting the dinner.

'Sometimes I forget that when you are little, it is never too cold to eat ice cream.

'Sometimes I forget that my children don't understand why I have to "do jobs" and why we sometimes just have to go somewhere, right now.

'Sometimes I forget that when you are little, it is much more exciting to hide under the kitchen table than to brush your teeth.

'Sometimes I forget that it is quite a long walk to the village shops when you have little legs.

'Sometimes I forget all these things. But today, as my children ran off enthusiastically to say hi to their new friends and strode confidently into their respective new schools, I remembered.

'So I thought I would write them down, to share with you.'

Hazel Gaynor

Hot Cross Mum, hotcrossmum.bogspot.com

Chapter 5: Behaviour and discipline

In this chapter we're looking at the best way to respond to your toddler's behaviour as a whole – tantrums get a whole chapter to themselves (chapter 7)!

- Why is discipline important?
- What is appropriate discipline for a child of this age?
- How do you get your child to listen to what you tell them, especially when it's 'no'?
- Should you smack?
- What sort of discipline techniques have worked for other parents?

Mind your language

If you think that a particular behaviour is not what you want, be careful to label the behaviour and not the child. 'That is a naughty thing to do' is very different to 'You're naughty'. The reason why we make this distinction (and it is an important one) is that if you label the child, then you risk creating a self-fulfilling prophecy. Tell someone they're naughty often enough and they'll believe it, and start to act accordingly.

In contrast, if you talk about their behaviour in the third person – 'a naughty thing' – then it is less a part of them, and therefore not an intrinsic part of their personality. A behaviour is something that can be changed – a personality less so.

So if you're thinking of putting your child in one of those 'Here Comes Trouble' T-shirts – stop and think before you do. Is that really what you want to create?

These might seem like minor points of language, but language can be a crucial part of how you relate to your child. This is why many parents and nurseries don't use the word 'naughty' at all, and instead get specific about what the child has done wrong and what the consequences of that are, i.e. 'When you bit Max it hurt him and made him cry' etc.

The flip side of this is to also get specific when praising your child's positive behaviour, rather than labelling everything you like as 'good', i.e. 'That was lovely sharing when you gave the toy to Isabella' etc.

I wish someone had told me to encourage rather than be negative
'When my two were toddlers I often found myself telling them "no", "don't touch that", "don't do this" … it goes on, and I am sure many people can relate to that. Now I prefer to follow the "five-a-day" habit.

'This five-a-day challenge doesn't relate to fruit and veg, but to encouragement. From such a young age our children look for attention. Whether this is positive or negative that doesn't matter to them, attention is attention, and children will naturally repeat whatever behaviour came just before the attention. So the more positive attention you can give from a young age the better.

'Catch your toddler red handed at good behaviour. This could be eating the food they have been given, playing quietly with a toy, playing together with another child, sharing something, showing love towards a sibling. No matter how simple the behaviour, the key is to acknowledge and give attention for something good, and naturally your little one will repeat this behaviour to receive more of your positive reinforcement. This is something I wish I focused on more when my two children were toddlers. Here's an example of five-a-day:

1) Well done for giving that to your sister.
2) I love you because you are kind.
3) Yay! You ate all your peas!
4) Great job sitting nicely.
5) Sitting with your toddler to look at a story, big cuddles and showing lots of love.

'What you focus on is what you get more of, so by creating a habit of saying at least five positive things a day and focusing as much as you can on the positive, you will see much more of the same.'
Tarryn Hunt
Mums That Care, mumsthatcare.com

Be a parent, not a pal

I really despair when I hear parents referring to their child as their 'best friend'. You are not their best friend, or they yours, and if you honestly think that that's the case, both of you need to get out more.

Why would a three year old want to be best friends with a 30-something woman? Why would a grown man get his friendship needs from a little kid? Your child needs a parent not a best friend. They can go to nursery and make plenty of friends. But at home, they need a parent.

You might think that you stepped into the parent role when you had your baby, but did you really? I think that we only fully step up to the parenting role once our children start challenging that role – when we have to be strong enough to say 'no' to them, and set boundaries.

Many of us find it hard to discipline our children – it seems too much like being the boring grown up, when we might not feel particularly grown up at any age. Also, this issue can cast a shadow back to our own childhoods, especially if our parents treated us in a way that we didn't like. Shouting at children and smacking them was much more acceptable to previous generations than it is right now. We have to find new ways of doing things and forge our own path.

When to discipline

You might think your child is a holy terror, but how naughty are they really? Often toddlers behave in a way that adults find unacceptable, but to the toddler makes perfect sense as part of their urge to express themselves and discover the world. So what if I smear this paint on the wall? It feels nice to do it... I'm tired, I'm crying, I didn't want to come to this wedding anyway... I hate that food, I think I'm gonna FREAK OUT etc.

So if your toddler's behaviour is off whack, think about to what extent you contributed to that situation and how you could have avoided it. Were they tired and due a nap? Are they picking up on stress at home? Was their blood sugar low and what they really needed was a snack? Was the situation basically pretty dull for a three year old?

Often you can draw a direct line from so-called 'naughty' behaviour to its causes. If you address the causes then you will address the behaviour. And if you strip back these identifiable causes, the times when your child is simply badly behaved for the heck of it are probably much fewer than you realise.

By thinking ahead to the situations you go into, you can often divert challenging behaviour before it starts. Expect the best from your toddler, but at the same time manage your expectations and don't blame your child if it all goes fruit loops at an inconvenient moment.

But even then, with the best will in the world, there will be times when your toddler's behaviour puts you all to shame. And that's the time when you need to show that their behaviour does have boundaries. Solid boundaries help children feel secure, but often they will check that those boundaries are in place by kicking out against them. So you owe it to your child to apply some discipline when it's needed.

What worked for us – Always follow through
'Discipline is always a tricky one. With my girls, I did try the tap on the leg approach but quickly realised that it had very little effect. So, I resorted to "the naughty step" when they were under three and from there on in, it has

been toys, play days, treats and so on being denied. I still have the same philosophy now with both my girls and it has worked brilliantly.

'It has to be said that it isn't easy to see it through and can be very challenging for a parent but it has to be done!! I can remember my eldest missing out on her sister's gymnastic party because she had been so naughty and had been warned of the consequences but I think was testing our boundaries. It was awful to have to follow it through but it certainly never happened again and Harriet very quickly realised that my word was gospel!'
Tracy Cazaly, mother of two girls
familyparentsgirlsdevon.blogspot.com

Smacking

There are many alternatives to approaching the same situation. Every family is unique and how each of us does things is our own business. But there's one issue on which I'm unequivocal – smacking. I don't do it, I think it's wrong and I don't want you to do it either.

I have never smacked either of my two children. And it's not as if I haven't wanted to. Sometimes I've felt so wound up by their behaviour that I could feel the mists rising and I wanted to let it out in a short, sharp shock.

But that is exactly what is wrong with smacking – all too often it's about the adult expressing their anger, rather than what may be best or most meaningful to the child. And the truth is that a smack is meaningless to a child. In fact it's contradictory. How can you tell your child not to hit others if you hit them? You are their greatest role model in everything, so model how you want them to behave.

If my children ever whacked each other (and it doesn't happen often), I say 'This is not a hitting house. I don't hit you, you don't hit me, and you don't hit each other'. We're all clear on the boundaries, and we all stick to them.

Find other ways to discipline your child and keep your hands to yourself. Walk away if you need to – sometimes parents can benefit from Time Out too.

Other methods of discipline
Time Out
Using Time Out (TO) or the Naughty Step has grown in popularity in recent years thanks to the *Supernanny* TV programme – it felt like Supernannny used TO in pretty much every house she went in to.

This is how it works: Find a safe, neutral spot which you designate the Time Out zone. It needs to be somewhere fairly boring, so it could be a corner of your living room or the bottom step of your stairs. Children have so many toys these days that being sent to their room is no great hardship. You can even buy Time Out Rugs from specialist retailers.

Give your child a warning if you're going to put them into TO – don't just bung them in there at the first sign of insurrection. Give them a chance to change their behaviour.

Put them in the TO spot for a short period of time. A minute for each year of their life is plenty and will feel like much longer to them. For the child, the punishment here is the lack of attention from you and the sense of being set apart from the rest of the family. If you use this method, you'll probably find it works best for older toddlers as most two year olds won't know what's up, unless they've seen TO being used with an older sibling, in which case they might be delighted at the treat of being regarded as a big boy or girl.

Counting to three
Personally I have had much better results with the counting to three method. This is similar to TO in that it gives your child a chance to pause and change their behaviour. It also has the advantage that you can use it anywhere, which given most toddlers' propensity to kick off in public, you might need.

All it really consists of is giving your child a warning that if they don't do X (name the behaviour you want them to change) by the time you count to three, then you will do Y. Never ever threaten something if you're not prepared to carry it out because your child won't take any future threats seriously. You must, must, must follow through on what you say you are going to do – this shows your child that the boundaries are firm and that they can believe what you say.

Remove favourite toy

I know some parents find this a bit mean, but it is effective. Children always have a favourite toy of the moment which they will not want to be parted from. Don't threaten to chuck it away forever – forever has no meaning for your toddler. Toddlers live in the moment, and right now is what they know and understand, so saying they can't have it today is going to be a bigger deal than if you say it'll be gone forever.

What will have an impact is if you remove the favourite toy and place it somewhere that your child can see but not reach. This teaches your child that negative behaviour leads to negative consequences. Give a warning before you do this to enable the child to change or stop their behaviour.

Sticker charts

Discipline can be administered via the carrot as well as the stick. For some reason, stickers are like a Class A drug to a young child – they simply cannot get enough of them. Stickers work particularly well with the under fives because they're such a visual tool – your child can see the rewards mounting up. Encourage your child to make an effort to earn a sticker, but don't make it too hard so that they can get some sense of achievement.

Advice for single parents of toddlers

Christine Lewandowski runs the *Single With Kids* website (www.singlewithkids.co.uk). She believes that the rules are similar for married and single parents where child raising is concerned, and a child can grow up happy and balanced as long as they have love and attention. This is Christine's advice for anyone raising a child / toddler as a single parent:

- There is a slight advantage in one parent raising a toddler in that it's easier to have consistency inside the home. A toddler needs firm rules and it's much easier to keep these consistent if they don't change from parent to parent;

- A happy parent helps raise a happy child. If mum (or dad) is stressed, tired or anxious then this can not only be picked up by the toddler, but can also affect the parent's patience and ability to cope with a demanding young child. It's essential for the parent to make sure they have some time to recharge each day, even if it's just 30 minutes soaking in the bath before bedtime. The chores can wait, sanity can't;

- Seek support – especially if you're a first time mum or dad. Toddlers are challenging and often break all the expectations we had of having children. Unfortunately the days of extended families have long since gone and there's often no one on hand to help, even more so if you're home alone with the child. Local Children's Centres can be a great starting point, there are also a lot of online communities such as www.MumsNet.com, www.NetMums.com and, specifically for single parents, www.SingleWithKids.co.uk, where a parent can seek a wealth of advice and chat to others in similar situations;

- DON'T see any low points in your child's behaviour (and there will be many!) as a factor of being a single parent. Toddlers are challenging and will have tantrums. This is simply a case of testing boundaries and exercising their new independence;

- DON'T feel you need to overcompensate for your marital situation with your little one. Many children have been raised by single parents from baby age and have lived to tell the tale (successfully too!) If you let a guilt complex flavour your parenting skills, you could make a rod for your own back – it's important to establish boundaries for your child and stick with them;

- Don't be afraid to ask for help. People are often afraid of offering in case it offends but are more than happy to lend a hand if required. Ask and take any time off offered.

How do I get my child to listen when I say 'no'?
Why won't these children just snap to attention when we tell them what to do? Anyone would think they weren't listening to us. When we say 'no' to our children, essentially we're saying two quite distinct things:

1. Stop what you're doing.
2. Do something else instead.

Which is a lot to expect from a child who's barely out of nappies. So you will make life much easier for both of you if, instead of saying 'no', you cut to step 2 and tell your child what you want them to do instead, e.g. instead of 'No jumping on the sofa' say 'The sofa is for sitting' or 'Jumping is for the floor'.

Anything we say repeatedly to our children, quickly becomes a load of 'Blah blah blah' to them and they do stop paying attention. I know of one mother who was very quick to say no to her baby, and when the child started to speak her first words were 'No' and 'Stop that'. But she never actually did obey her mum. If you want your child to obey you, you need to do more than just say 'no'.

So as much as possible, tell them what you want them to do rather than what you don't.

If you hold back on the negatives, they'll take more notice of them when you do say 'no'. When you feel yourself about to say no, ask yourself what you'd prefer your child to do and tell them that instead. This'll make it easier for them to change behaviour because you'll be giving more options. It also naturally draws your child's attention to the behaviour you want, rather than what you don't want. So, for example, if your child's a scrapper, rather than talking about the hitting, talk about the kind of behaviour you want to encourage – friendliness, gentle hands etc.

And whilst it might be easy to remember the challenging behaviour of our toddlers, they've got masses of good points too. If you do decide to focus on accenting the positive, you won't have to look far for stuff to praise I promise.

> *I wish someone had told me about the climbing*
> 'The one thing I wish someone had told me about toddlers? I wish I'd known about their innate skill for climbing. Every one of my kids reached the point where if there was a handhold within reach they would be on top of a wardrobe the minute you turned your back. Forget keeping valuables out of reach, it is the steps and shelves you need to watch. Of course the sheer joy on their face when they're doing it means there is no way on this earth you'll ever get them into trouble for it. Our youngest has worked out how to climb up firemen's poles at the swing park. She's only two! Of course after climbing out of a third floor kitchen window onto the window ledge when I was 18 months old I should have expected it ...
>
> 'The one thing I wish someone had told me about toddlers is that they can out grump the old guy that lives on your street that chases the kids away, puts a knife through every football that lands in his garden and tells every kid the truth about Santa. The furrowed brow, the huff of the shoulders and the pettied lip. You just can't look at them without bursting out in laughter, which of course just makes them worse. I can only imagine this is the practice run for their teenage years.'
> Bob, father of four
> *Wisdom Begins in Wonder*, wisdombeginsinwonder.com

Key points about discipline and the under fives:

- Never give in or respond to tantrums or they will only get worse;
- Challenging behaviour in toddlers has many identifiable roots – it's not simply about naughtiness;
- Be careful to label the behaviour, not the child;
- Your child will feel more secure when they know boundaries are in place;
- Tell your child what you want them to do, rather than simply saying 'No';
- Both parents need to be consistent with discipline – whether they're together or not;
- Not all toddler behaviour is bad!

Why I love my toddler

'I was once told that two year olds are not deliberately difficult, they just make mistakes. I'm not always convinced – particularly when I say "don't wake your sister" and she proceeds to shout in her loudest voice. We give her a hard press sometimes but always come back to how gorgeous she is. It's often difficult to focus on the positives but in reality there are lots of lovely things about two year olds.

'There's the pride that they show when they achieve things – my daughter beams and says "I did it". As difficult as it may be to let her do things herself, especially when we are in a rush it's wonderful to see her achieve things.

'Though often toddlers like to challenge us and do the opposite of what we say, they also love being helpful. If you give my daughter and her friend a special job to do they are eager to help. She is good at tidying up, putting things in the bin, helping put the washing in the machine and feeding the dogs.

'She is incredibly loving. She loves to have hugs and often says "I love you" and wakes me in the morning with a hug and a kiss. I love hearing her laugh – she is incredibly ticklish and it's lovely to hear her unrestrained laughter.

'I love that she is learning new things all the time and her beaming smile when she discovers something new. I love reading stories with her. She has had a love of books from before she was a year old and is always asking for stories. When she is getting difficult because she is tired she will sit and cuddle in to you sharing her favourite books. It's also lovely to see her "reading" books for herself – reciting the well-known phrases verbatim. If you give her a book with single words accompanied by a picture she believes she can read and looks so impressed.

'I often find myself hoping that the two's will soon end in the hope that we will have a more civilised little girl. Writing this has reminded me of all the lovely things about her and that sometimes I should take a step back and remember those things.

'Children grow up so quickly and soon these times will have been and gone and I'll wish I had appreciated them more.'

Rachel McClary, mother of three
www.rightfromthestart.wordpress.com

Chapter 6: Potty training

Moving from using nappies to a grown up toilet has got plenty of potential for angst, but equally can turn out to be relatively straightforward – so long as you keep it calm, don't rush it and have always fancied improving your skills at cleaning pee off the floor. In this chapter we're looking at:

- How do you know when your child is ready for potty training?
- How do you start potty training?
- When can you expect dry nights?
- Poo problems and what to do about them.

Do not rush it

When my daughter was a toddler, she was very chatty and seemed quite advanced for her age. So when, just after she turned two, I was advised by child carers to start potty training, I agreed. The only trouble was, my daughter didn't.

On and on it went for months – countless accidents and mopping up wee. I think we finally got there in the end with reliably dry days at just over two and a half.

By the time my son turned two, three years had passed. This time I decided to take a different approach and follow rather than try to lead him into potty training. I bought a couple of potties around the time he turned two, and whilst we had them around the house, we didn't make a big deal of it. If he wanted to sit, he sat, and got plenty of praise for it. I didn't do anything to encourage the process and left it up to him to tell me when he wanted to ditch the nappies and move into big boy pants.

And the funny thing was – the outcome was the same, and he was also dry at two years and seven months. But the process was far, far swifter and simpler and took less than a week from start to finish. It turned out that by leaving it later and not forcing the issue, potty training became much easier.

> *What worked for us – Follow the leader*
> 'It's better to follow your child's lead. We tried to push Kayleigh thinking she was "ready" and it was awful for us all. When she was ready she was dry through the day in three days.'
> Paula Fazekas
> *Mummy vs Work*, mummyvswork.co.uk

You don't need a pot to potty train

Whilst this chapter refers to 'potty training', since that's what most people tend to do, there's no rule that says you 'have' to use a potty. Some parents (and indeed children) prefer to go straight to using a regular toilet. This is absolutely fine, and if this is what you want to do, you'll find special loo seat inserts available in shops to make them easier for little bums to use. All of the advice in this chapter will apply regardless of which method you use.

And if you are using potties, get several – at least one for each bathroom your child will be using. Trust me, carrying a steaming pot full of wee around the house is best avoided. Plus if your child gets used to 'going' near to the toilet, that's one step closer to using the loo itself.

How much training is really going on here?

In a lot of ways you're not really training the child, but rather helping them gain awareness of their own bodily functions. Your child needs to learn that a particular feeling in their body means that they need to pee or poop. There's no way you the adult can show them that – they have to learn it for themselves. Girls are often potty trained earlier than boys, but there is no cast iron rule to this.

What you can do is encourage – be positive and reward their efforts with praise. You can help with routine by putting your child on the potty after meals and at regular intervals throughout the day. Just don't get anxious about it – if you start trying to potty train but your child isn't interested, stop because they're telling you they're not ready. Try again in six to eight weeks and you might see a big difference.

Bribery

This probably puts me in the Bad Parent Corner, but I did reward/bribe both my children with Smarties when we were potty training. Basically, it was a deposit for a deposit – put something in the potty and you get a choccie of your choice. And once they were established out of nappies, we mysteriously ran out of Smarties. So shoot me. At least it worked.

> *What worked for us – Chocolate buttons and a special loo seat*
> 'We knew Kieran was ready because he was taking his pull-offs down and doing his business on the floor. He hated the potty so we bought a padded seat for small bottoms to go onto the "Big" toilet. This worked fantastically and tied in well with being a "big boy".
> 'Chocolate buttons were a great tool for toilet training too. For every successful wee or poo in the toilet there was a reward. One button per success. Very quickly he didn't want a button but more the praise of doing his business like a big boy.'
> Nicki Cawood, mother of two
> curlyandcandid.co.uk

Plan for potty training

The preparation stage for potty training is longer than you might think. Plenty of parents optimistically buy their two year olds a birthday present of a potty and some snazzy pants, but it can be a long while before they actually get used as the manufacturer intended.

So much of the potty training experience is new to your child that you need to start things off in a very low key way. So they wants to wear their pants on their head? That's fine. Sitting on the potty whilst still wearing a nappy? A great start. Sitting is, after all, the first part of the process, and your plastic pot may start its life as a story telling chair rather than a bodily waste receptacle. It's all good, it's all moving in the right direction.

What you are aiming for is for your child to be comfortable with these things, to feel ownership of them and to want to use them. When it comes to pants, look for whoever is your child's favourite book or TV character and get undercrackers with those on. I know that some parents don't like to see their child in licensed clothing but you'll find it useful to ease up on this one. Not wanting to pee on Thomas the Tank Engine's head could be the vital element when it comes to your child staying dry.

How do I know my child is ready for potty training?
The signs for this are very clear, and have nothing to do with age, so don't feel that if your child has got to a certain age that they 'should' be out of nappies. These things vary a lot from child to child, even within the same family. Signs to watch out for before you start potty training:

• Talking about it.
Does your child seem aware when they need to go, and do they tell you? Do they know that they've had a pee or a poo? A child needs to know the difference between feeling wet and dry, and you can't force this.

• Increasing dryness.
Does their nappy stay dry for around 2–3 hours at a time? Do you ever go to change them and find that the nappy is still dry, or less used than you'd expect? This could be a signal that it's time

to let your child run around without a nappy or wearing those precious new pants.

• Motivation.

Do they want to? Does your child see other children using the loo or potty and want to do it too? Are they interested in becoming a bit more grown up? Are they happy to sit on the toilet or potty for at least a few minutes at a time?

• Timing.

Can you devote a few days to potty training, when you're at home or close to home as much as possible? There's no point in starting when you're about to go on holiday or need to be out and about a lot. Plan to start when you know you can be at home and physically close to your child for at least the first couple of days.

> *I wish someone had told me you can't force it*
> Nicola Seary is a mother of five who says it feels like she's always had a toddler:
> 'As a mum of five you'd think I'd be an expert by now. I have to admit I'm not. This is one area which I have found difficult. I have tried all sorts of potties and toilet seats. I've started or attempted to start toilet training with all of my children when they reach 2 years old to no avail. Three has so far been the age when I have success-fully managed to toilet train my children. I think our youngest will probably be earlier though as he wants to copy everything his older siblings do. My children are growing up so fast.'
> Nicola Seary
> www.compchatandkids.wordpress.com

Tools of the trade

One of the easiest things you can do to get started with potty training is to swap daytime nappies for pull-up pants. These are a slightly thinner type of nappy which the child pulls on like pants, so it gets them used to doing that. You can still pull them apart at the sides for changing purposes.

Also, once you've actually started potty training, when you're dressing your child, make it as easy as possible for them to get on to the potty if they want to. So go for loose fit clothes such as jogging trousers or loose dresses that they can pull on and off easily. Avoid things like trousers with complicated fasteners, tights or dungarees. Or if it's the summer – nothing at all!

Plan to be at home as much as you can for the first few days of potty training. And you will have to be as physically close to your child as possible, ready to whip that potty under their bum at the first sign of action.

And odd as it may sound, this is why potty training can be a very special time for parent and child, as you stick close together for days at a stretch. It's a particular type of one to one attention, a (hopefully) never to be repeated time, so try to enjoy it – at least the bits where you're not wiping up poo from places where it ought not to be. That bit is a struggle to appreciate for even the most dedicated of parent.

Some people feel that there is no going back once you have ditched the nappies, but if you really feel you need to stop and postpone, there's no harm in this.

For boys, it's probably easier all round to start them off wee-ing sitting down – it'll be a while before they can get it together to pee standing up. And they'll probably pick this up from other boys or their dad. It's a skill that seems to come naturally, though if you think they need target practice then a table tennis ball or a scrunched up wad of paper down the loo makes a good target.

I wish someone had told me they all get there eventually
'My three year old son has taken the best part of a year to train. He would happily sit in his wet clothes all day rather than tell me he needed a wee. He gets too wrapped up in watching TV or playing with his Nintendo DS to think about practicalities like toilets!

'I literally tried everything – ignoring it, shouting, hovering round with a potty, being casual but watchful – you name it! I eventually got over this and got him aware of his body by observing when he has a drink then literally taking him to the loo 30 minutes later – whether he needed it or not, to "have a try".

'Sometimes this worked, sometimes it didn't, but after every successful wee, I'd high five him and make a big fuss about what a good boy he is to get him wanting to use the toilet. When he did have an accident I'd just change him into clean clothes without any fuss but no praise either. It took time, patience and mountains of washing but we are there now – eventually! I make sure I always have a change of clothes for him in my bag and some wet wipes, plus an empty drinks bottle on hand for him to pee in if we are not outside or otherwise near a toilet.

'My son is still not dry at night but I'm relaxed about this – it was more important to me that he was dry for nursery. The night time stage will come in its own time. There is no pressure on this, he's only three (almost four).'

Nadine Hill

JuggleMum.com

Accidents happen

Nobody gets through potty training unscathed. Don't fool yourself to think that you can survive this stage without scooping up a bit of pee and poop off the floor. My daughter used to pee for effect. I could watch her all day, but as soon as my attention was elsewhere (Phone how dare you ring!), there she would be, smiling as she soaked up the carpet. My son used to have accidents because he was so engrossed in something way more important, like play – I would find him sitting playing with his cars, bum-deep in a pile of poop that he hadn't even noticed. Thanks kids, you're the gift that keeps on giving.

Stay close to home as much as you can when you're potty training and always take a change of clothing for your child when you go out. But if you forget, you'll cope. You won't have been the first parent to have to dash into the shops to buy their child full set of clothes from the waist down. I remember once cringing when my daughter produced a puddle on the floor of the children's books section in Waterstones. I shamefully went up to the cash desk to let the assistant know, but she was fine about it and airily said 'Thanks for letting me know, most people don't bother'. As with many milestones in your child's life, what seems momentous to you is fairly run of the mill to other people (and my daughter has gone on to be a regular customer at Waterstones, so karma-wise I think it's evened out).

Buy a bigger handbag

A portable potty can be very useful when you're at the transition stage – you can buy some that fold up very flat and use disposable liners. You may need to carry one with you if your child is still getting to grips with a full sized toilet. This doesn't mean you can whip it out in any occasion – I was once asked to leave the library for inappropriate use of the portapotty, but what can I say? It was my first time potty training. We're all inclined to be a little stupid sometimes, and I am reporting back these mistakes so you don't make them too. Other places that use of the portapotty is likely to be discouraged include: restaurants; churches and the runway at Heathrow Airport. Just aim to be sensible and considerate of others is all I'm saying.

Of course, Toddler's Law dictates that the day you leave home without a potty is the day that your child will announce their need to wee in the most inconvenient of circumstances. Don't take it personally, it's what they do

For such situations your options include an emergency plastic bag, behind a tree or diving into the nearest fast food place.

When do they become dry at night?
This varies hugely from child to child. Some children become dry during the day and at night at pretty much the same time, whilst others are still wearing night time nappies for years after they stopped needing them the rest of the time.

Around one in seven children start school still in nappies at night. Doctors don't generally consider this a problem unless a child is around seven and still wetting the bed. So whilst hopefully your child will be potty trained by around three-ish, they may have some time to go before they get there at night. It's not something you can make happen because your child needs to be physically ready. And it doesn't seem to have much to do with the size of your child – I have known very big children who were still wearing night nappies at five and beyond. It's one of those many parenting issues that we just don't talk about – not many parents will strike up conversation at the school gate by telling you that their child wet the bed last night. But it does happen, it's very common, and you're far from alone if it's happening with your child. What won't help is putting pressure on the child – in fact, it just might make the situation worse. But there are some things you can do:

- Watch out for your child waking up with a dry nappy. A run of three or four of these and you may be ready to do without;
- Make it easy for your child to find the loo at night. Leave a light on, or use a torch, or you could even leave a potty by the bed;
- Consider limiting bedtime drinks. Does your child still have a bottle or a big drink of milk at bedtime? Cut back on this, and avoid fizzy drinks and anything with caffeine altogether;
- Increase drinks at other times. This will help to encourage the bladder to function well during the day.

What worked for us – Waiting
'My five year old daughter is finally getting rid of the night time pants this weekend after three weeks of dry nights.

'I know this is quite old but she's never been consistent with her dryness before even though she was day dry by two and a half, it was nights that were proving difficult for her. I was initially worried, after all my son was dry day and night at three, but finally just took the view that there aren't many 18 year olds I know putting their bedtime pants on, so she'll lose them when she's ready! And after a very long wait she's finally done it!'
Natalie Donohoe
livi lou & dude, lilioudude.blogspot.com

What if they won't poo in the potty?
Some children don't like to poop in the potty and will hang on until they have their night time nappy on to make a deposit. Believe it or not, this is actually very common. It's one of those subjects like nits or piles that many parents have to deal with, but very few discuss. So rest assured that this is a normal phase which many children experience, and not related to anything you have or haven't done. And like all phases it will pass, so be patient.

Your child may seem to be physically ready and recognise the physical sensation when number two is coming, but emotionally still wants to hold on to the nappies and doesn't want to let them go just yet.

Here are a few options for ways to approach it if your child seems reluctant to ditch the nappies:

• Do nothing.
  Stick with the nappies or pull-up pants and trust that your toddler will move out of them when they're ready. If you're still using them in six month's time, reassess.
• Use a sticker chart to encourage more use of the loo or potty. Stickers are a very effective motivational tool for boys and girls under five. My daughter used to put a sticker on her potty every time she used it. My son needed a bit more of an incentive, so he got to choose a new toy when he'd managed

to keep the Number 2s in the loo for a week. Use which ever motivational tool you think your child will respond to.

- Stop buying pull-up pants or nappies.
  Going cold turkey is a more drastic approach which may result in a few tears and some mess, but if you don't have them in the house then they can't be used. Obviously this won't work if your child still needs them at night.
- Use your older children as role models.
  Talk to your toddler about what it was like when your older children were potty training. Get your child to tell you how they feel about it, especially the bits they don't like and feel anxious about. Try not to pressurise and focus on using the potty or loo as an achievement to be proud of.

Deliberate soiling

Some children, whilst they may be happy to wee in the toilet or potty, still have a habit of pooing in their pants. It ain't pretty, but there you go. If you react with horror at the discovery of a little something extra in your three year old's undergarments, rest assured that you're not the first parent to have to deal with this, and you certainly won't be the last.

Again, it's a common phase and it does pass. Some experts link this behaviour with a fear of independence. You can help your child by watching out for when they need the loo, perhaps sitting them on it after meal times.

Make sure your child's diet contains enough fibre so that they're not likely to get constipated – plenty of bananas, oranges etc. Above all stay as relaxed as possible around the whole issue and offer plenty of praise when a poo does reach its intended destination.

Should you let your child see you on the loo?

Actually, this is something you may not have much choice about, since toddlers are seldom respecters of the closed bathroom door. And by the time your child is a toddler, the luxury of going to the toilet by yourself may have become a distant memory anyway. But if your child is fearful of potty training, this could be a good opportunity to teach them that going to the loo is something we all do. Either that or get an adult accessible lock for the door.

Key points about potty training:
- You can't force it, you can only encourage when your child is ready;
- The signs of readiness are very clear and easy to spot;
- Only attempt potty training when you have a few days clear at home with no other distractions;
- Night time dryness can take a long time to follow day time training – doctors don't consider this a problem until the child is at least seven;
- Many children start school still in night time nappies;
- Refusal to poo in the potty or loo is an extremely common phase that will pass.

What I love about toddlers
'1. They wake up happy.
Toddlers don't wake up and say "ugh, don't want to get up yet", groan, and roll over. Toddlers wake up full to bursting with energy and what's the first thing they want to do? They want to see you. Can you honestly say, hand on heart, that anyone else in your life is pleased to see you every single morning? Toddlers – they're the living embodiment of *Carpe Diem*.

2. Their needs are simple.
Cuddles? Check. Breakfast? Check. Toys? Check. Cuddles? Check. Cheesy macaroni? Check. Cuddles? Check.

3. Chubby legs.
Those fleshy pins are just about the most adorable thing in the world and before you know it, bam, they're gone. When else are you going to be proud of having a kid with fat legs?

4. Time and weather.
They don't know what day it is, they don't know what time it is, and frankly they don't care. They only know that it's either 1. Playtime or 2. Time for Lunch. Plus, they don't care what the weather's doing, they pretty much want go outside anyway.

5. Colouring in.
It's often the number one indoor activity for a toddler, but have you ever done it with them? Have you sat down, crayon in hand and worked hard to stay within the lines? It's surprisingly therapeutic.'
Alex, mother of two toddlers
littlemissmadamandthesunshineduke.blogspot.com

Chapter 7: Dealing with tantrums

In this chapter we look at probably the loudest and most well known toddler behaviour – the tantrum. In particular:
- Why do tantrums happen?
- What do I do when my toddler erupts in the cereal aisle of the supermarket on a Saturday afternoon?
- Does every child have tantrums – and should I be worried if mine doesn't?
- The benefits of tantrums (yes there are some, you just have to look closely).

Toddlers have a bit of a bum deal when it comes to tantrums, because if we're being honest, people from the age of two to ninety-two are just as capable of throwing a wobbly when life doesn't go their way.

And if you don't want tantruming to get your own way to become a lifelong character trait, you need to think very carefully about how you approach it now. Put simply: if your child gets the message that screaming and stomping their foot gets them what they want, they're going to keep doing it, even into adulthood. Is that the kind of person you want to raise?

Why do toddlers have tantrums?
The best way to think of a tantrum is like a show or performance. Your child is expressing how they feel in the most basic way possible. They don't yet have the skills to hold back or express themselves in a different way. Anger and frustration collide and the result can be fairly startling.

But every show needs an audience and this is where we parents come in. Sometimes the most effective way to deal with tantrums is to ignore them – literally leave the room and pay attention to something else. This will also have the effect of distracting them as they'll wonder what you're up to. Distraction is one of the best behaviour management techniques for this age group.

Tantrums are normal!

Author Hollie Smith has written nine books about parenting, including *Cool, Calm Parent* and *Toddling to Ten*. She wants to reassure parents that tantrums are a normal part of the process:

'Tantrums are totally natural, and totally to be expected, and I think it's important that parents realise that (particularly first-timers – the benefit of experience will usually render you blasé about the tantrums of subsequent kids), because a truly spectacular toddler-wobbler can actually be quite alarming.

'I remember being horrified by some of the early paddies my daughter threw when she was a toddler, to the point where I sometimes wondered if she had behavioural issues! It wasn't until later that I realised it was normal – healthy even!

'But if you don't know that, you can feel like the worst parent in the world when it happens – especially if it happens in public, with the audible tutting of (usually aged) witnesses ringing in your ears. In fact, to this day, I still get a tingling sense of relief – as well as a rush of empathy – when I witness a little kid losing it in public, because it's NOT MINE!

'Mainly, toddlers throw tantrums because they're frustrated. They're old enough to know what they want, but they may not have the language skills or the physical ability to achieve it – or maybe they're just not allowed it, and naturally, that pisses them off.

'And at that age, they just don't have very well developed anger management skills. These will – for most of us, hopefully – come with time, particularly once they start going to nursery or pre-school and learning about appropriate ways of responding when life doesn't go their way.'

True Confessions – My worst tantrum
Here are some of the reasons parents told me that their child had had a tantrum:

- I had cut his sandwiches into triangles and he wanted squares;
- He only wanted to wear green, but the green top was in the wash (mainly because he'd been wearing it for a week non-stop);
- Her favourite TV programme had finished;
- I wouldn't let her play with my glasses;
- You put her socks on the 'wrong' feet – every morning. Oddly, Granny manages to get it right;
- The ice cream had the temerity to MELT;
- Daddy couldn't fix the stick that broke;
- His sister has chicken pox and he doesn't;
- The toilet seat was too cold.

So whilst sometimes you can anticipate and avoid a tantrum before it starts, at other times – well, there ain't a lot you can do. Though even with the most random of tantrum triggers, you may be able to detect their root in tiredness, boredom, frustration or hunger – or all of the above. It's an impulsive reaction.

But if we look again at the list above, I think there is a common thread – it's all about control. Your toddler is coming to terms with the fact that they're not in control of much of their world. And this makes them ANGRY.

In time they will learn to handle this, plus they will start to get a bit more control as they become more independent. But for now – well, you can see how a growing realisation that somebody else calls the shots of every aspect of your life would kind of tick you off, wouldn't it?

I'm a control freak!

So when you're tackling tantrums, one way to approach it is to let your child have more control and choice over their lives. So maybe you choose their outfit, but they have the last word on shoes and undies. Or maybe they choose it all, because they'll soon learn that a sundress won't work in November.

Ignore, rather than engage with the behaviour you don't want to encourage.

Show that you have high behaviour standards, but at the same time respect your child's individuality. Look for ways for your child to have at least a little control over their life, whilst still retaining over all authority yourself – keep the basic boundaries firm.

Stay strong – don't waver. Never ever give in to a tantrum or you will be storing up problems for future behaviour. Giving in teaches your child that histrionics will get them what they want. As I used to say to my kids (repeatedly) 'Crying and shouting gets you nothing'. Your child needs to learn what sort of behaviour does and doesn't bring rewards (and a parent's undivided attention – even negative attention when you're telling them off – counts as a reward, which is why you need to ignore tantrums).

Sometimes giving in to your child can be a way to achieve peace in the short term – very tempting, particularly with public tantrums. But it is a short term gain with long term consequences. So for the sake of future tantrums – don't waver with the one that's happening now.*

*OK, yes, I know you will. We all do it sometimes. Don't feel bad about it, we're all allowed a couple of strikes out. The trouble is, the more inconsistency you show your child, the more confusing it is for them.

What worked for us – A four point plan
'When Louie was two and he threw his first almighty tantrum, I stood completely thrown as he thrashed about on the floor screaming. I came home and read

everything I could about how to deal with this behaviour, and this is what I found worked:

Distract: 'Look there's a bird, flower, cloud, dinosaur" (ok there's probably not going to be a dinosaur). Whatever interests your toddler that you can draw their attention to in that moment to get them to forget the urge to throw a strop.

Ignore: If distract isn't working then the best thing to do is ignore the behaviour. If you're at home and your child is safe, walk away. If I'm in public and my child is safe I usually just turn away. I honestly don't care what other people think, after all they were once (probably) toddlers, screaming and kicking on the floor themselves.

Comfort: I find that when a tantrum reaches a certain point, and you will know when, because you know your child way better than I, go in with a cuddle. My son at that point would gladly cuddle me and calm himself down.

Praise: When the child has calmed down praise them for calming down. When the child meets the same situation next time and doesn't throw a tantrum, praise them for being so good.

These tips only work if you stay calm. On the occasions when I have used my other parenting technique of losing my cool and muttering expletives, the response from both the children and onlookers has not been as good.'

Ella Tabb, mother of three
purplemum.com.

Make way for a tornado coming through

Sometimes, particularly with epic, tornado-like tantrums that just need to blow themselves out, you will need to put your child aside in a safe place such as their bedroom. Once they get to that whirling dervish, arched back state, your child is so caught up in the moment that they've probably forgotten what it was that made them angry in the first place. So for the sake of both you and your child's sanity, give them a space to calm down.

It doesn't need to be for long – hopefully less than 10 minutes should be enough – and afterwards simply carry on with your day rather than rehashing where things went wrong. Ten seconds after the tantrum's finished, your child will probably have forgotten all about it, so follow their lead.

> *What worked for us – Time Out*
> 'My daughter would throw her head backwards when having a tantrum so I would lay her on the floor for a time out. Let her get the tantrum out of her system whilst knowing she wasn't going to bang her head on something. Sometimes children just need to get the frustration out (although embarrassing for us mums) they are usually happier afterwards.'
> Boo
> boorootiggertoo.blogspot.com

No tantrums here – does that mean I'm a better parent?

Not necessarily. Maybe you're just good at avoiding them. Maybe your child is saving them up for puberty. And neither does it mean somebody whose child has a lot of tantrums is a bad parent. Sometimes that's just how it works out.

Though age two is known as 'Terrible Twos', many parents (myself included) find that their child's worst meltdowns don't happen until they're around three or older. So if you've sailed past two with barely a cross word, don't smugly think that you've had a narrow escape and passed the worst that other parents suffer. Your time may well still come.

> *What worked for us – Avoidance and running shoes*
> 'I'm lucky in that I haven't had too many toddler tantrums in supermarkets to deal with. How have I

achieved this? Shopping online mostly! When I have had to take Cormac to the shops, I've found that moving fast is the key to success. And I mean really fast. Also I've brought various entertaining or tasty things with me to distract him. Sometimes letting him ride in the trolley helps.'

Ellen Arnison
In A Bun Dance, bundance.blogspot.com

I wish someone had told me about the terrible threes
Anonymous blogging mum *BarenakedMummy* has found that with her two children tantrums have peaked at three rather than two:

'They all warn you about the terrible twos but no one warned me about the terrors of turning three. With both girls, I've had to use different strategies for dealing with tantrums. (Yes, it's military planning here!)

'Bel didn't really tantrum much – she was possibly the perfect first child, which obviously spoilt me when Car was born. When she had done something wrong we could put her into time out on the naughty step and it worked. I also remember that when she looked as if a tantrum was brewing we'd distract her.

'When Little Miss Butter Wouldn't Melt Car starts, well, God help you. I've tried the naughty step and she will literally throw herself off it! And the noise, it doesn't half give you and possibly everyone else a headache!

'So, what do I do? Well, I've resorted to counting, one… two… three… four… five…

'I can on good days get to two and she will stop. But sometimes, even the counting doesn't help and then we do have to send her to her room or take something away.

'Remember if you are dealing with a tantrum, here are my handy hints:

'DISTRACTION – even the most inane objects can be used;
'NAUGHTY STEP – if your child is small, try and hold them but watch out you may be kicked, bitten etc;
'COUNT – slowly and calmly;
'Of course, if all else fails there is always the option of passing the children to your other half, taking a deep breath and heading for the nearest glass of white wine!'
www.barenakedmummy.blogspot.com

Pick your battles

Neither you nor your child would be happy if you were to point out every little time their behaviour goes adrift. You would end up exhausted and they would have low self-esteem.

Don't pick your child up on every little thing they do wrong. Yes, have absolutes like no hitting or biting, but there will be times when you can let the minor stuff slide.

Don't wade in straight away with bickering siblings or friends. Give them a chance to work it out themselves. Save your energy for the big things and let the rest of it roll off you like water off a duck's back.

Twin toddlers – twice as many trantrums?
'Toddler twins might well have given me double the trouble my friends had, but I found the terrible twos passed by relatively easily because the children always had each other as a distraction. One of the best ways to diffuse a toddler tantrum is by praising the non-tantruming twin – it's amazing how quickly the badly-behaved one calms down! Ignoring tantrums is always a good tactic, and that's so much easier when you've got another child there to focus your attentions on.'
Emily Carlisle
morethanjustamother.com

The benefits of tantrums

Yes, believe it or not there are benefits to tantrums. Children gain security from having firm boundaries put in place. And one of the ways that they check that those boundaries exist is by kicking out against them – sometimes literally. So the fact that your child feels secure enough to express themselves is a good sign, and healthier than bottling it all up.

> *I wish someone had told me you can't put toddlers on eBay*
> 'My son has just hit the "terrible twos" and I am completely at a loss with him. Yesterday I even considered putting him on eBay but I thought I'd probably get bad feedback once they received him! Seriously, I don't know what to do with him. Yesterday the tantrum was all because I said it was time to put his pyjamas on – completely unreasonable behaviour from me!
>
> 'I've never seen anyone get so angry. He ended up frothing at the mouth and I was scared he would have a fit. I tried holding him tight, sitting at the end of his bed, trying to reason with him, leaving the room. Nothing worked. It lasted 45 minutes. I ended up reading him *No matter what* about a grumpy little fox whose Mum loved him "no matter what". At the end he burst into tears and gave me a hug. Love that boy. Bring on tonight!'
> Sian, mother of two
> *You're Not From Round Here*, offcumden.blogspot.com

Calming the storm

Leading UK children's hypnotherapist Lynda Hudson has these tips:

> 'Remember, no single solution works all of the time but some of these ideas work some of the time! Obviously solutions may depend on the particular situation you find yourself in. How you respond in the middle of the

supermarket and how you respond at home may be very different but here are a few ideas.

In general, remember that tantrums are a toddler's way of expressing frustration and getting attention. They are not really old enough to express their frustration in a more appropriate way; after all they probably don't even fully understand why they are so cross or jealous and they don't have the sophistication of thought or verbal ability to express themselves in a more adult manner. At this point in their development they are creatures of feelings, not considered thought processes! Sometimes, they really need a hug or sometimes they just need to be given a little time ... just like grown-ups really!

• Distract them.

Children are renowned for being able to switch from mood to mood at the speed of light. Sometimes, a "prove me wrong" technique will be effective such as "I bet you can't start smiling by the time I count to ten" and then slowly count from one to ten and (if you can!) smile yourself as you do it. Smiling is infectious!

• Do something quite different to surprise them.

It almost doesn't matter what – start to jump about / sing a song / wave your hands in the air. This type of response can work really well but use it judiciously and occasionally. It's the surprise element which gives it its positive effect! Or a kiss and a cuddle is a great idea.

• Stop yourself from shouting!

Remember that you are their role model and they will copy you.

• Walk away.

Or just take a physical step back so you can calm down yourself and be less involved in the emotion of the moment. Counting to ten also works pretty well! Walk away so they get less attention for the tantrum behaviour and, once they have calmed down, go back and give them a hug and some praise for having calmed down.

Praise them for beginning to calm down, even if it is just a tiny bit or even if they are just pausing to take a breath. It rewards and encourages the calming behaviour. Remind them of how to calm down e.g. take a big deep breath; count their fingers if they can.

Make an effort to use positive language rather than negative e.g. Say "Speak quietly so I can understand you" instead of "Stop shouting" or "Don't scream at me like that". Generally this has a more calming effect in itself.

Ask "are you feeling good now? Are you feeling happy now?" (shake of the head) then ask "wouldn't you rather being doing x or y right now" (a nice thing) which starts to reduce the tantrum's energy.

Generally a tantrum is a way of getting attention. Think about this later on your own when you are away from the emotion of the tantrum. What was behind it? Were they over tired? Feeling left out? Hungry? Totally bored? Could your expectations of their patience have been a bit too high for their age and development? Could there be anything you could do differently in a similar situation to avoid a tantrum occurring?'
Lynda Hudson
www.firstwayforward.com

Public performances – should I care what people think?
In a word – 'No'. Toddlers aren't especially choosy when it comes to picking a time to have a tantrum. And they're very good at picking up on their parents' moods. So if you are in a hurry and trying to get the shopping done, or distracted by an important

phone call or getting ready to go out, your child can pick up on this and react in a way to reclaim your attention. Often there's an exponential effect – the more you need your toddler to be quiet and calm, the louder they will crank up the decibels. Insurance company on the phone = no reaction. Your boss calls to discuss an incredibly important and sensitive work project = wailing loud enough to wake the dead.

When your toddler kicks off in a public place, it's easy to feel self conscious, as if other people are judging us. The truth is that they're probably not. Or if they are – well, more fool them. If someone judges other people, it doesn't define those people, it simply defines the judger as someone who needs to judge.

I'm not suggesting that you ignore other people entirely. If your child has a meltdown in a restaurant or somewhere where there are other people with a reasonable expectation of peace, then of course you should take other people's feelings into consideration. Be aware of the ecology of the situation. If you suspect that your child is disturbing others, remove them from the situation and deal with it elsewhere.

But remember that as parents, we've all been there or are going through it too. Strangers may look at you because they feel sympathetic, or relieved that it's not happening to them, not because they're judging you.

Often when our child has a public tantrum, we may behave in a way that we wouldn't at home – you might lose your temper, resort to bribery or sheer begging. It's not a failure if you do. All parents resort to desperate measures at times – sometimes you just have to do what you can to keep going. At home, you might have the strength to ignore a full-on meltdown, but when it's happening at 5pm in the baked beans aisle and all you want to do is get home, that's another story.

Aim to keep your attitude to tantrums as consistent as you can. Think about strategies you will use when out and about – because you will have to deal with a public tantrum one day. Strategies you use at home, such as Time Out or ignoring, simply may not be practical elsewhere. Start ignoring your child and walking away from them in a public place and someone may call social services.

Things start to get tricky with public tantrums when the people you're with start to stick their oar in, probably just when you need it least. Other parents will have their own strategies for dealing with tantrums, and your Mother-in-Law may start to chime in with how they did it 'In my day'.

Resist the urge to snap back at anyone who gives you unsolicited advice when it comes to dealing with your child. They mean well. They're trying to help. And perhaps they will help – especially if they see how life is with a toddler and that you could do with some support.

What worked for us – Absolute firmness and ignoring onlookers
'Tantrums, I just am very firm back to her.

'She sat on the floor in Tesco recently and I was not in the mood. So I went down to her level and said "This is not going to wash today young lady, get up or you get no treats later". Yes she got up but the crying continued. People stare at you but it really does not bother me. I think everyone else has their opinion but every child is very different as I have experienced with my two.

'Amélie can scream and I mean scream, for 20 minutes at a time to get her own way. I totally ignore her, do things around her like make a cup of tea or do the washing so she can see I am totally ignoring her. In the end she stops, walks over to me and apologises and we talk about what happened.

'This took a while to get to this stage and believe me, the screaming can make me want to scream too but I cannot let her take over the house and she needs to know who is in charge.

'On the other hand she is a creative, happy child. She loves to play with her dolls and can happily make up stories about what is going on with them. I bake with her

too and use that as a treat after good behaviour so that she starts to understand the difference.'
Michelle Hanlon, mother of two
www.michellehanlon.blogspot.com

What worked for us – Stay calm in the face of adversity
'When my daughter had her first meltdown in the supermarket, I decided the plan of action was just to leave it to fizzle out, so I plonked her in the trolley (after a bit of a fight) and carried on shopping with her screaming and grunting away. I'm sure by this point there was probably people tutting and thinking to themselves I can't control my daughter, but I was in full control (or so I kept telling myself!)

'What were my other options? Abandon the shopping and run out? Give in and let her have what she wants? Or be nicely nice so she gets her own way in the end?

'So off we packed our shopping with her screaming and by this point Ethan had joined in for the fun of it. Then I proceeded to our car and packed our shopping, with her still screaming and this carried on till we got home. So I put her straight to bed and let her scream it off, telling her in the process that it was not acceptable and I did not wish to see or speak to her until she had calmed down and apologised.

'A full 50 minutes after the tantrum started it ended, with an apology.

'Then our day continued with a lovely lunch out for just the three of us (and maybe I was a bit frazzled but I wasn't prepared to admit that).'
Paula Fazekas
Mummy vs Work, mummyvswork.co.uk

Strategies for dealing with public tantrums

These strategies can be applied in any situation:

1) Plan ahead – think carefully before you go out about the possible tantrum potential. Are you close to a nap time? Is your child likely to be hungry? Will you be doing something very boring that your toddler won't be interested in? As your child gets older, you won't always have to plan things to this degree. But when they're at the toddler stage it helps and you'll be glad you did.

2) Distraction – distraction is probably your greatest weapon when it comes to dealing with the open air tantruming toddler. This is why God invented little tiny toys that fit in your handbag, and raisins.

3) Remove your child from the situation – yes you may have to wolf down your meal or miss it altogether and change plans at the last minute, but often you are better off cutting your losses and removing your toddler – this will have the effect of distracting them as well.

Key points when dealing with tantrums:

• Tantrums are a natural part of development;
• Think ahead and anticipate tantrum triggers before you start;
• Ignoring the tantrum and distracting your toddler works best;
• Be firm and consistent in not rewarding tantrums;
• Sometimes you just have to let a tantrum blow itself out;
• Don't take it personally – they're not doing it deliberately to wind you up. At least if they are, they'll never admit it.

Why I love my toddlers
'The really delicious thing about toddlers is their enthusiasm for life and their appetite for new experiences. I can see why grandparents go ga-ga for toddlers, because often as a parent you don't realise at the time that toddlerhood is quite a fleeting stage – in a few short years

your kid will be capable of saying 'I hate you Mum' and can refuse hugs – but toddlers are endlessly affectionate, want to share every tiny sensation and experience with you, and that stage when they start communicating in sentences is absolutely magical.

'Write down all the funny things they said or did because you'll regret it otherwise, and you'll be amazed at how much you'll forget.'
Heidi Scrimgeour, mother of two
heidiscrimgeour.com

Chapter 8: Siblings and introducing your toddler to a new baby

Children under five will often have to cope with the transition of moving from being the only child in the family to the arrival of a new baby. Or maybe your toddler's having to assert their identity amongst other siblings already in residence. So in this chapter we're looking at brothers and sisters, and how the arrival of a sibling might affect your toddler:

- What's the best way to manage the transition from one child to two?
- What's the best age gap to leave?
- How do toddlers react when a new baby comes along?
- How to tell your toddler that there's a new baby on the way
- How should you handle it if your toddler isn't happy about the arrival of a sibling?
- What happens if not one, but two new babies arrive?

What's the right age gap between children?
Two point seven six years. Anything else and your child will turn out dreadfully warped and mangled.

OK, only joking.

There's a straightforward answer to this one, because the truth is that there's no such thing as the best age gap, just as there's no such thing as the 'right' age to have a baby. It's a question of what works best for your family, plus how much your body is willing to get with the programme.

My daughter was three and a half when I had my son and that felt like the right age gap for us. I didn't have to deal with two children in nappies at the same time, and my daughter had her own established life and friends which continued, so it's not like everything had to change for her when the baby came along.

Some parents I know who've had a very close age gap have complained that they didn't have enough time alone with their eldest before the next one was on the way. Others say that a close age gap has worked just fine for them, as it means that their children are going through the same stages in fairly close succession and can become good friends in the process.

And of course, for many of us the age gap between siblings is determined by fertility and how long it takes you to get pregnant – something over which we have little control. So as much as we may agonise as to when to add to our families, the truth is that you might as well not bother.

If you are considering having another child, trust your instinct and don't over-think it too much. There are always 'What ifs?' when it comes to major life decisions, and you could drive yourself mad trying to consider them all. Just accept that whatever age gap you end up with it will turn out to be the right one for your family.

What worked for us – A large age gap
Michelle Hanlon has two children with an eight year age gap:
'My girls are aged 11 years and 3 years old. They were/are very different toddlers, not sure if it's me or their personalities!

'I was only 20 when I had my first, Olivia, and I think that must have changed the way I parented. I was not as mature the first time round. I have had to adapt my parenting for Amélie as she is a much more demanding child.

'The relationship between the two girls can be strained and can be lovely. Olivia plays beautifully with Amélie sometimes but if she is in a mood or wants to stop playing, then it will erupt into an argument. Olivia

thinks Amélie gets all the attention so even though she is older, the rivalry is still there.'
Michelle Hanlon
michellehanlon.blogspot.com

What worked for us – A small age gap
Lauren Goodchild has a much closer age gap to handle, with two boys under two:
'Naively, when I was pregnant with Spike I thought that my very easy going, 21 month old toddler would be ecstatic to have a baby brother. When I was 20 weeks pregnant we moved and started living with the Hubby full time. Spud thought it was great and he has so much fun with his daddy. We were a lot closer to extended family so saw them more often which Spud thought was great because Nana and Pops are the bees' knees! We had a great thing going on.

'Add a baby to the mix and you get this:
'Spud was NOT happy. He visited me in hospital and was so curious and loving with his baby brother, I was thrilled. He wasn't thrilled when the baby came home with me! He was even less thrilled when the baby went to visit his Nana and Pops. He wasn't treated differently by anybody. I still had one on one time with him, doing everything that he loved and I was so adamant that people weren't even allowed to look at the baby until they had spoken to Spud that quite often Spike got left in the corner! To Spud this didn't matter, he ignored anybody that was holding the baby, it was as if he was looking straight through the person, pretending they weren't even there!

'Back at our home things were easier with just the four of us and he did have some lovely moments where he would give the baby a cuddle or give him his dummy but it was very much on his terms. If he didn't want to he made damn sure that we knew about it! It made having two children a lot harder because I was totally split between them.'

So as much as you can think that things are going to be OK, life doesn't always go to plan. But Lauren found that despite the initial problems, life as a family of four did improve:

'Over the weeks Spud got used to the fact that Spike wasn't going anywhere. We caught him giving him the evil eye like he is plotting something but so far Spike has survived the wrath of his big brother. Not that he ever noticed that Spud had an intense dislike for him, Spike has always been in total awe of his big brother and probably always will be.

'Six months down the line and we have a very loving, helpful big brother. If he is tired or clingy then it is still very much on his terms and to get photos of them together either has to be done in stealth mode or with chocolate bribery.

'I know that our age gap will be amazing when they are older and every day it gets better but I really wasn't prepared for the early days and the possibility that it wouldn't all be plain sailing!'
Lauren Goodchild
spudandspike.co.uk

How to tell your toddler that there's a new baby on the way
Nine months is a long, long time when you're little, particularly when you're a toddler who tends to live in the moment anyway.

So avoid telling your toddler about the new baby too early – it won't have much meaning and they will be wondering why the baby isn't here RIGHT NOW. Wait until they start asking you if you've been eating all the fairy cakes.

Pregnancy with a toddler

I had my son when my daughter was three, and a pretty full on Threenager at that. When I was pregnant I pretty much carried on as normal. It was incredibly different from my first pregnancy, when I spent rather too much time on the sofa stroking my bump and gazing wistfully into the middle distance.

Pregnancy with a toddler in tow is a whole other kettle of fishcakes. Your attention is much more on the child in front of you rather than the child inside of you. Consequently the pregnancy may fly by in super quick time.

Being heavily pregnant or with a newborn baby plus a toddler may turn out to be a bigger challenge than you might expect. Your toddler will be full of their usual rambunctious energy, whilst just getting out of bed is a challenge for you.

I wish someone had told me how easy having a toddler and a new born would be

'There is a five year gap between my eldest and middle child but I fell pregnant again when my daughter was 18 months old and was dreading having two children so close together.

'We never expected to have three children, had only planned on two so my daughter for the first eighteen months of her life had been spoilt and treated like our last with Mummy doing everything! So to find out she would become a middle child and have to make way for another baby really made me worry. But once he was born I realised that actually having two little ones close together was in fact easier than having a big gap.

'The great thing is that now they have grown up, they play happily together and occupy each other and last year when my daughter started school, my little man missed her terribly as he had no one at home to instigate the play and boss him around!'

Kizzy Bass

mummyneeds.wordpress.com

Toddler reactions to a new baby
The arrival of a new brother or sister, whilst welcome, will also rock your toddler's world. It would be unusual if they didn't respond to that change in some way. These are some of the reactions you may see:
- Increased clinginess;
- Regression in potty training;
- More tantrums;
- Fussiness over food;
- Night waking.

So basically, brace yourself for uber-toddler, with all the tough stuff ramped up to the max. And you may also find that reactions like these start to happen during your pregnancy, as toddlers are very quick to spot that your attention isn't 100% on them.

Essentially this behaviour is all about asserting your child's claim on your undivided attention, and reinforcing their genuinely held belief that it really is all about them – which is why, ultimately, one of the best lessons having a sibling teaches a child is that the world does not revolve around them and that other people's needs deserve consideration too.

I remember when my son was newborn, feeling slightly helpless that I was pinned to the sofa in pretty much nonstop breastfeeding mode, whilst my daughter roamed around the house getting increasingly feral. All the active things we had done previously like baking and painting had to go by the wayside. Even getting out to the shops with the two of them was an ordeal. For the parent of a toddler, having a new baby is a time of adjustment too. You may still be thinking of your eldest child as a baby, but now you can see just how much they've grown.

What worked for us – A special box of toys
Emily Carlisle's son was just becoming a toddler when not one, but two siblings arrived. She found that the adjustment was smoother than she expected:

'My son was fifteen months old when his twin sisters arrived. Although he was really too little to understand much about the pregnancy we talked lots about the new babies and he helped me get their clothes ready and sort out toys they might like.

'As he still used a muslin cloth as a comforter, we bought new ones in a different colour from the girls, so there could be no confusion. When the babies arrived we called them "his" babies and asked him to help lots – checking which one was crying, or showing visitors where the twins' room was. He was very proud of them and never appeared to be jealous.

'The hardest part was when I was breastfeeding and couldn't play with him. I put together a special box of treats which I would get out only during a feed. The box contained books, a story tape and special toys which kept him occupied for half an hour or so. When the feed was finished the box would go away again until the next time. It worked really well, in fact often he would tell me to feed the babies so he could play with his special toys!'
Emily Carlisle
www.MorethanJustaMother.com

What worked for us – Thinking corner technique
Seema Thobhani is mother to two girls and director of *Kidz4Mation*, a company which produces workshops and resources designed to boost confidence in children:
'My daughters, now aged seven and five, definitely went through sibling rivalry. When I was expecting my younger daughter my husband and I explained nicely to my older one about what's going to happen but that didn't stop the older one troubling the baby… we were quite stressed in those days. We used to apply the "thinking corner" technique which worked, we praised her, I spent more time with her and eventually we saw a decrease in the behaviour.

'Thinking corner is a technique still used by us whenever we need to discipline them. Whenever we see an unacceptable behaviour from them they are given a warning. For example, "This is a warning, next time I see you do that you will go to the thinking corner". Then if they repeat the unacceptable behavior, one of us take them into a corner and they stand there for the number of minutes equivalent to their age. Whilst putting them in the corner very calmly I would kneel down (get to their eye level) and say, "You will stand here for five minutes because of what you did (specify the behaviour that was unacceptable) and think about it" then leave from there.

'On returning after five minutes, kneel down again and they'll say, "Sorry Mum I won't do it (should specify the behaviour that was unacceptable) again" then I would give her a hug and bring her back to the room. If her behaviour was unkind towards her sister or anyone she should say sorry to them. When they are younger they won't be able to say much but they will realise that their unacceptable behaviour will have consequences. Consistency is the key here.'
Seema Thobhani
www.Kidz4Mation.com

I wish someone had told me to do nothing

Tania Sullivan is a mother of nine who at the time of writing is also pregnant with twins. She somehow finds time to write about her life at largerfamilylife.com and is the sort of person for whom the phrase 'I don't know how she does it' was invented. This is Tania's well-practiced advice on how to prepare your toddler for the arrival of a new baby:

'I've been there and I want to reassure you that it doesn't have to be difficult or complicated. It's really quite simple and it works along the lines of two words:

'Do nothing.

'Ok, so it's not actually quite that simple. It's more like three words:

'Do nothing much.

'The largest age gap between my children is five years and four months. The smallest is just over 11½ months. With my first child I was very worried. He was only a baby himself and was about to be shunted out of the way to create room for a new baby. Or at least, that's how I looked at it. A 14 month old isn't a great communicator. I couldn't explain the changes that were about to happen and I couldn't reason with him. I followed all the tips that the parenting magazines and books gave.

'I took to carrying a doll around in order to prepare him for the new baby and so he would get used to seeing me holding somebody else. I would talk to him all the time about the new baby. All the time. ALL THE TIME. I went into talking overdrive. I bought a present for him which was specially from the new baby. She would give it to him when she was born.

'I did all the things the experts told me to do and when B-Day came and she was born the result was... nothing. He was fourteen months old. He came to see us in hospital and was more concerned with his shoes. The doll was another toy to play with and I think he probably took as much notice of my incessant chatter about the new baby as he did when I talked about anything else. Very little.

'He was fourteen months old. He got on with it. Within a week I doubt he even remembered not ever having his baby sister about. I fussed, I worried and I stressed. He lived life and took it all as it came.

'After that I relaxed. I didn't fuss, I didn't over-talk the "new baby is coming soon" conversations with them (or in the younger children's cases, at them) and I didn't bother with gifts from the new baby.

'We would tell them that a new baby is on the way and then leave it. If they mentioned it we'd talk about it but only in passing. No more overkill of, "Are you going to love the new baby? Are you? Are you? ARE YOU?!" We just stopped stressing and worrying.

'They would see us get something out for the baby. A steriliser, a bottle, a blanket for example. A conversation might come about on what it's for and then they'll go and play and that is it. No more. No less.

'When each baby has arrived we have had no issues at all with jealousy from any sibling because from the start it has been treated as nothing out of the ordinary. I truly believe that the reason that no child has reacted negatively to a new baby is because they haven't picked up that there might be a need to react. They don't expect a clash of thunder and lightning and for their whole world as they know it to change and so they don't react as though it has.

'By treating it as something that is a little different but still normal, not out of the ordinary and something that doesn't merit worry or concern in any shape or form, the toddler will do what toddlers do and that is to just get on with life. Toddlers are more concerned with their food, their own nappy and their toys. Honestly, we're the ones who try to second guess what they are feeling about the new baby and the truth is that they don't care. It's just another day of their life to them.

'When your toddler needs a kiss or a hug or to climb into your lap it isn't down to jealousy, it's because he's doing what he always did. This time you're noticing it because you may be busy tending to the baby and there-fore not instantly available like you were before. To sud-denly label the toddler as being jealous is not fair when they are only doing what they have always done. He still needs his kisses and cuddles and time just as he always did. He doesn't understand that it might not be a convenient time and you are now busy with someone or something else. He just knows that he's always called the shots and they were answered immediately and now they're not and he doesn't get why.

'So my advice in a nutshell: Do nothing much. Talk a bit but not much. If toddler wants to join in "helping" let him. If he doesn't, don't push him. Don't treat the impending arrival as a potential threat or major change to his way of life. If he thinks it's not a big deal then he'll treat it as such. And please don't label him as being jealous for doing what he's always done. He's going to seem big and grown up to you overnight. To him, he's just who he always was. Mummy's little boy. Or girl.'

Tania Sullivan
www.largerfamilylife.com

Key points about siblings:
- There's no such thing as the 'best' age gap;
- The arrival of a new baby will very likely affect your toddler's behavior;
- This behaviour change is temporary and your toddler will soon adjust and probably forget life before the new baby pretty quickly;
- Don't assume that introducing a new sibling will inevitably mean trouble, because it will mean a lot of joy as well.

Why I love my toddler – The big sister
'Lola, my almost two year old, has been anything but fun lately. Everything is a battle: from getting her in the car seat to choosing a pair of socks. When I read her a story, she pulls my ponytail. When I change her nappy, her naked bum is off down the hallway before I can stuff her into a clean one. When her dad kisses her goodbye in the morning she pinches his double chins, both of them. She steals her big sister's crayons (and writes on my walls).

Yesterday she tried to bite her other sister's arm. She is challenging. She is difficult. She is a tornado of destruction wreaking havoc on all our lives. No one in our family is safe from the wrath of Lola.

'Except perhaps for one.

'Lance. Her baby brother, fourteen months her junior.

'Around Lance she is the sweetest little mummy you ever saw. He lies on his play mat and she brings him toys. He fusses and she hands him a dummy. He howls in his highchair and she fetches his teething ring from the fridge. He cries in the double stroller on the way to pick up the big ones from school and she leans over to give him his bottle of milk. She even kisses the top of his head when she thinks no one is watching.

'I have days when Lola makes me want to scream, days when I am counting down the minutes to her bedtime from her first meltdown of the day. But when I see her with her baby brother, my heart explodes with love. For however much she tests my patience, however frustrating and impossible I find her to be with, I've seen a glimpse of the beautiful, caring, loving soul that lies beneath her feisty exterior.'

Anonymous mum
Almost Bedtime, 12hourstobedtime.blogspot.com

Chapter 9: Looking after yourself

In this chapter we turn our attention to a child's greatest role models – their parents. Yes, that's you. No, I know you didn't sign up to be a role model, but for better or worse, to your child that's what you are. So what kind of a role model do you want to be? The frazzled kind? Or the slightly more chilled kind, who sees that her needs aren't of any less value than everyone else's? So let's look at:

- What can you do for yourself as a parent when your day is dominated by the demands of a toddler?
- Is it possible to have a bit of 'me time' or is that just a pipe dream for now?
- How can you feel calmer if your toddler is driving you crazy?

'Me Time' is one of those maligned phrases that has come to be derided as much as it is desired. It can feel like yet another obligation to add to your list – a list which is probably already full to bursting with things you don't have the time or energy to get round to as it is.

So how achievable is it for the parent of a toddler to have some time to yourself, to have a life away from your child? Is it worth the bother?

When I asked parents of toddlers this question, they looked at me as if I'd gone a bit squiffy in the head and asked me if I was feeling alright. 'Me Time, what's that?' just about sums it up. And yet, if you dig a bit deeper, some parents do carve out pockets of time for themselves. Some run or go the gym, some get crafty and make things, others blog, join book groups, get involved in charity work or simply relax with a glass of wine in the bath at night. All of them are just as busy as you, so if some people can do it, it must, by definition, be at least possible. But with more than enough on our plates already, why should we bother?

Why looking after yourself is a necessity, not a luxury

Now, since this is a book all about toddlers – those scrumptious, infuriating, demanding and lovable little darlings – you might be wondering what a chapter about parents is doing in this book on toddlers. After all, it's not as if there's a shortage of things to say about the under-fives, is there? We could be here all day.

But I believe that taking care of yourself is part and parcel of taking care of your child. Because as we've already discussed, children, even little babies, are very sensitive to their environment. They're like a barometer of your life.

So if you're stressed, worried or rushed off your feet, they will know about it, even if they can't say it (To be fair, they may be the cause of it). If your relationship is troubled, even if you never argue in front of your child, they will pick up on it.

This is why, when your attention is elsewhere, your child's behaviour may react against this. They sense that your attention is not with them, so they want it back.

So given that our child's moods and our own are so intertwined, it makes sense to see taking care of yourself as being part of taking care of your child. You're not being a better parent if you sit on all your needs, and end up feeling unfulfilled. Happy parents = happy kids. It's all interlinked.

What worked for us – Getting outside
'As a mother who has experienced post natal depression, making sure that I stay on top of things with my emotions is a must. I have a very lively four year old and I would need to make sure that we did go out or have some sort of activity planned both for my state of mind and her rising energy levels. I make sure that we are outside walking in the field or with friends as friendships are very important in helping on the days that you feel down. A problem

shared certainly rings true, and never feel that you will be judged because friends don't do that. Exercise is also very important, that was my way of getting pampered – I like running or gym classes.'
Angeline Brunel, mother of one
daftmamma.co.uk

Step away from the iron!
Your child will never thank you if you martyr yourself to them and make parenthood your only interest. And don't use lack of childcare as an excuse, because there are always ways around that – apart from paying a babysitter, you could do childcare swaps with another parent. Or you could take up an interest that doesn't require childcare – anything from reading, playing video games to running your own online business. And if all else fails, there's always drinking and sex (not at the same time though, unless you are particularly ambidextrous).

And don't make housework an excuse either because that one's never going to go away. There will always be more dust to hoover, but in the scale of things our lives are pretty brief.

So that is what this chapter is about – the importance of looking after yourself, and suggestions as to how you can practically do that, give that your time is more than likely very squeezed already.

I believe that the time we spend away from our children is what helps us be better parents when we are back in the bosom of our families. Even if it's only a few minutes with the bathroom door locked, you need that breathing space for the sake of your own mental health. You need time when you're something else other than someone's mum or dad, and don't have to think about whose bottom needs wiping.

What worked for us – Militancy and timetabling
'I have to be militant with my "me time". After I realised that I was feeling guilty if I ever took time out for myself,

I have been stricter with myself. At the beginning of each week I write my to-do list for the week, and then I schedule a time to do each thing, drawing up a timetable for the week. But I always make sure to include free time for myself in this schedule. It's up to me how I spend it, but mostly I try to turn off the computer and read a book or watch trash telly.'
Heather Young, mother of twin toddlers
Young & Younger, youngandyounger.net

Pleasures shouldn't be guilty
Men seem so much better at taking time for themselves than women do. They sail off for Saturday morning football practice without even a backward glance. Why is this? Why don't women sail off on Saturday afternoon and do the same?

Because of the dreaded guilt, that's why. And if you want to make life manageable for yourself as a parent, you need to get rid of the guilt as soon as you can.

What is guilt? The feeling that you're not doing it well enough, not being a good enough parent. Well, you probably are. If your children are happy and reasonably healthy, and not picking scabs off each other's heads, you're doing a good job.

Keep calm and carry on
Clinical hypnotherapist Lynda Hudson has this advice for parents who want to feel calm in the face of toddler madness (www.firstwayforward.com):

- Only where it is safe to do so, give yourself a break by walking away from the emotional situation for a few moments or a few minutes so you can regain your equilibrium;
- Remind yourself of an occasion where you have looked at them and been filled with love or pride;
- Vigorously shake your frustration out of your arms and hands. Movement helps let go of stress hormones stored in the body;

- Notice where the tension is in your body and systematically let the different muscles relax. Or, tense them up even more first and then consciously let them go imagining a rag doll;
- Breathe out the tension and take some calming deep breaths;
- Use your imagination for a two minute daydream. Drift off to a beach or a favourite place for a couple of minutes and imagine letting all stresses and strains go;
- Speak to yourself firmly and remind yourself that tantrums are a phase and they will grow out of them;
- Ask yourself how important this is on a scale of serious life events;
- Again, giving them a cuddle even when you don't feel like it can restore happiness all around;
- Tell yourself you can cope well enough. You don't have to be perfect!
- An excellent way of calming yourself is to listen to a relaxing / calming hypnotherapy CD. You can put one on at night before you drift off to sleep and it really helps you cope in the daytime.

Unrealistic expectations

One very important thought to bear in mind is – your children will never have had enough of your time and attention. They are a bottomless pit in that respect. Whatever you do, they will always want more, and will protest if you try to take your attention elsewhere. Adults tend to emphasise quality time with their families, but to a small child quality time and quantity of time are exactly the same. You could give them your full attention 24 hours a day and it would still not be enough. So where does that leave you?

Some parents are entirely satisfied by family life and do not feel the need to look elsewhere for fulfilment. Those people are going to get a shock when one day their children grow up and leave home and there's a big empty hole in their lives.

Having a child is an enormous change in anyone's life, and the first few years can be incredibly physically as well as emotionally demanding. You may be existing on far less sleep than you ever did before, and it may be as much as you can do to get from the end of one day to the next.

Also there are practical considerations – what if you have no babysitters to call on? What if funds and time are limited?

Get in tune with your child's energy patterns

Nadine Hill of *Juggle Mum* is a time management expert and mother of a toddler. She believes that 'Me Time' isn't an impossible dream for the stretched-out parent of an under five – you just have to be creative and flexible about how you get it:

'In the 1970s when I was a child, I was allowed a freedom that children now don't have – and my parents had this freedom away from us kids too – to get their own rest.

'Nowadays we have to be ever present, our children don't get let out of our sight and we are always watching for choking hazards, sharp corners and to make sure they are "playing nice" and not pulling the cat's tail! It is necessary nowadays but it is also exhausting!

'But parents these days need time to re-charge their batteries, so they can continue to be the ever vigilant, "always on" nurturer they are. Too much self sacrifice without respite would turn anyone into a 'hard done by, put upon, shouty parent'.

'IDEAL SCENARIO: If you can get a grandparent or partner to take it in turns with you to take the kids off your hands so you can get a proper time out, you can go to the gym, sleep in or hit the shops. Whatever nurtures you is the activity you should do – NOT HOUSEWORK!

'However, if you don't have anyone to take the children off your hands for a couple of hours, the trick is to align yourself to their energy patterns. Children can be demanding but fortunately they lack stamina, so be in "alert" mode when they are at their most energetic, and take it down a notch when they are more sedentary.

'There is no shame in going to bed when they do at 7pm if this is what you need to catch up on your rest. If Mickey Mouse is on TV, cuddle them on the sofa and watch it with them. They just love having you close. If you really can't stand kids telly, cuddle them but have your iPod on to listen to your own music or read a book in your free arm (the other is round the child). The child won't know you are listening to Gangsta Rap whilst they are counting with Mickey – and you still get to go off into your own world for a short time to rest your eyes and re-charge.

'Take some self imposed pressure off. Use the technology we have these days to make your life easier. Order groceries online – let the delivery man take the strain of humping packs of potatoes around. Who needs to battle the supermarket and find a parking space with a toddler there to slow you down?

'Recognise that this period of your life is exhausting and it can be hard, but there is also a lot of loveliness to it – like having your chubby cheeked two year old sit on your knee and tell you she loves you.

'The best advice I can give is to roll with it – take each day as it comes and enjoy each moment. It goes so fast when you look back.'

Nadine's top five practical tips for carving out time for yourself are:
- Use your mobile phone's alarm function. If you have a half hour window to yourself before collecting a child, don't spend the whole half hour clock watching – you are wasting your own time. Set the alarm for the time you need to leave for the child and until it goes off, forget everything else but what you are doing. Be mindfully present with your me time – this helps you feel less rushed.

- Carry your MP3 player with you, loaded up with some tunes you love. Then, when you get five minutes, you can listen to your favourite track. Music has an ability to energise us or make us feel certain emotions with certain tracks, so have different playlists on your player so you can create the emotion you want to create in seconds. Have some kids music on there too so you can easily entertain them with songs they will like to get some peace and quiet!
- Use mobile video. If you have a smartphone, download whatever they watch to the player so you always have something to entertain them – helps if you're somewhere boring like a doctor's waiting room for example.
- Bathe with the kids. This doesn't sound much like 'me time', but it can be. If you get in the bath with the children at bath time, you can get a facemask on whilst you are in the bath, I bet you won't find the time or energy at any other time during the week to do that! Plus if you have a spouse around to take the child out to dry them afterwards, you can sneak an extra 5 minutes to yourself in the bath whilst they are getting them ready for bed.
- Use a slow cooker. It makes for a calmer tea time when kids are tired to have a casserole all prepared and ready to go, so you can spend the time before serving up either playing with kids or doing something of your choice, rather than being under pressure in the kitchen trying to pull together dinner for a certain time. Tempers are strained when people are tired and hungry so a meal that is ready when you are and has been gently cooking all day is a blessing on busy days.
  Nadine Hill
  www.jugglemum.com

Blogging – the hobby of choice for the 21st century parent
Blogging by and for parents has grown enormously around the world over the last few years. And some parents are even seeing this part time hobby grow into a full time job that they can work around their children and make a decent income from.

Why blog?

Parents blog for all sorts of reasons, each one as valid as the next.

- Tell your story for posterity.

  Perhaps you want to keep a record of these precious but fleeting times in your family's life. You can capture all the special moments, ready to look back on in the future.

- Keep wider family updated.

  If you live far away from your family, your blog can be a space to keep them updated with what's going on. You could use your blog to share pictures and videos of your life.

- A chance to get published and make your mark.

  Maybe you always wanted to be a writer, but never had the opportunity before. Your own blog is your chance to publish whatever you want to say, and work on your writing and storytelling style. Perhaps it will develop into a new career?

- Your blog can be a chance to connect with others.

  The worldwide parent blogging community is a friendly one, with regular meetups and events. Your blog could prove to be a way to connect with other parents and make new friends.

- It can be an extra source of income

  If your blog reaches a wide enough audience, you may want to start and sell advertising space or get paid for sponsored posts.

- It can be a space to work through life's frustrations.

  A blog can be written anonymously, and many are. So if you want a space to sound off about the things in your life that get you down, or make you happy or sad, this could be it.

- You can get free stuff.

  Marketeers are incredibly switched on to the influence of parent blogs these days. Established bloggers can find themselves over-run with offers of products to review and invitations to events. If this is what you're interested in, don't feel you have to say yes to everything, and don't make it the main reason why you blog. Concentrate on creating posts that you enjoy writing and the rest will follow.

Toddler blogging

Maria Jose Ovalle writes the blog *Mummy's Busy World*, from the point of view of her toddler:

'My son Matias (Little M) is only two and a half so he doesn't know what the blog is, but he does recognise himself on the computer screen and when he sees the blog header he says 'Matias's blog!' or 'My blog'.

'We do lots of activities together as a family and take plenty of pictures. Some of them make it on the blog and we have sat down scrolling through the posts. He recognises the pictures and he will tell me what was going on on that particular day when the photo was taken.

'I think when he is older he will look back on it kindly and enjoy it. The tone and approach I take is very innocent and I do try to capture what he could be thinking. Kids are honest with their emotions and very funny so I do try to keep to that. Oddly enough, writing from his point of view has brought me closer to him. I feel an even bigger connection when trying to see the world through his eyes. Thinking like him has actually made me take a closer look at my behaviour towards him and how what I do and say can and will affect him.

'There are plenty of blogs out there written from the child's point of view or as a diary of family life. What I would say to others is really think what your end goal is. Are you writing to advise others, keep a record of your family life etc? Would you be comfortable with your children reading your personal thoughts?

'There are all sorts of blogs and many parents have said they wouldn't want their children to read it. In my case, I can't wait for him to read it and see all of the joy he has brought to our lives and a glimpse of how we were with him. I really do love "our" blog – my husband gets involved too and we want Matias to be proud of it.'

Maria Jose Ovalle

www.mummysbusyworld.com

Getting started writing a parenting blog

Getting started blogging is incredibly easy and free – you'll find free templates at blogger.com or wordpress.com. The hardest part is deciding on your title and design, but the systems are very easy to follow and you can get going with very little technical know-how. If you get stuck at any point, Google your question and somebody, somewhere will have answered it.

There's a great community around parent blogging in the UK, which you'll find at networks including Brit Mums (www.britmums.com) and Blogger Ed (www.bloggered.co.uk).

Blogging about your toddler – points to consider

One good thing about having a toddler is that you will never be short of material for your blog. Whether it's recounting the story of their latest meltdown or recording the latest developmental milestone, there's always something to say. But does that mean that you should say it all?

- Think about your future child. I know it's hard to imagine, but your little pudgy bundle of adorableness will be an adult one day. And they may not thank you for telling the world about their potty training story. We are the first generation of parents who have to consider their children's future Google-ability. So how should we approach that?
- Don't use your child's real name when you're writing about them in your blog. Choose a nickname, initial or first name only. One day someone is going to Google your child's name – it could be an employer, partner, enemy or friend. Give your child the chance to create their own identity online.
- Be cautious about photographs. Avoid showing anything that identifies your child such as tops with the name of their nursery or school. Some bloggers don't show pictures that show their child's face clearly, but this is up to you. Your child may have the same name when they're an adult, but they won't have the same face.

- You can make your blog invitation-only. This means that it is not open to the public to view, and only people whom you've invited and who have the correct password can view it. Some bloggers choose to make only certain posts private, if they're writing about particularly sensitive or personal events.
- You can make your blog totally anonymous. This may be the best option if you are worried about what your mother-in-law may think.

And it's not even when your child is an adult that you need to think about – what if they start a blog themselves? I know several ten year olds (and younger) who blog. If you are treating the blog as your own private space to write about your life, remember that everyone you write about may one day read what you've written.

But despite these caveats, the rise in popularity of parent blogging shows that having a space to write about your life is a welcome one. It gets the stresses of life out of your head, down on to (virtual) paper and makes them more manageable.

Writing things down has a long history in personal development as a therapeutic tool – people used to do this in journals or diaries, and nowadays they often do it in a blog. If you have a lot of thoughts swirling around your head that you want to get perspective on, or simply a few funny stories to tell, writing them down will help, and blogging gives you the option to publish and share them with a wider audience. For more information about blogging and the support it can bring, read Ellen Arnison's book *Blogging for happiness: a guide to improving positive mental health (and wealth) from your blog.*

Key points about taking time for yourself:
- You have to recharge your batteries at some point, otherwise you end up running on empty;
- By taking care of yourself you are also taking care of your family;

- Blogging is a great option for parents who enjoy writing;
- You owe it to your toddler to be calm.

Why I love my toddler

'I love my toddler because when he's asleep he looks like a little snoring angel wrapped in a patchwork knitted blanket. When he's awake he runs me ragged and can either drive me a little crazy or amuse me endlessly. My little cute monster has been known to throw toilet paper downstairs when he's bored. Rather annoying, but very funny. I have wondered if he was an Andrex puppy in a former life. Little things like that keep the days interesting; you see I may be rushed off my feet, but life is never boring.

'I must be having fun because the time flies by in a rush of toast crumbs, cuddles, piles of washing and molehills of Lego in the living room – it seems like only yesterday when he was a tiny squeaking baby nestled in his Moses basket. Sometimes I sit with a cup of tea in hand watching him whirlwind around the house, spreading chaos and laughter and I'm so very thankful for his little life and the part that I have to play in it. On the other hand, I cringe because I know I'll have to clean all the mess up – but you have to take the rough with the smooth!

'Something I love about him too, is that he makes any walk into an adventure. He imagines bears or dragons hiding behind bushes and then fights them with imaginary swords, he pretends his hand is a spider and jumps it from wall to wall whilst chatting nonsense to it and he balances precariously on absolutely any wall or kerb he can find. I'm happy to toddle along beside him, pick him up when he falls over and run after him for as long as he needs me. Why do I love my toddler? Because he's my little ray of sunshine and my trouble bubble.'

Kay

Brink of Bedlam, brinkofbedlam.co.uk

Chapter 10: Preparing for nursery and school

It might seem premature to be thinking about school when your baby is barely out of nappies, but depending on when in the year your child's birthday is, they could be starting school when they've only just turned four. Or your child may be starting nursery and already making the move towards becoming a pre-schooler. And much as we might have tried to encourage you not to worry and to trust your own instinct, this move into the wider world does strike fear into even the most laid back of parent's hearts. So in this chapter we're looking at:

- Getting ready for nursery – how to minimise separation anxiety;
- As your toddler becomes a pre-schooler, how can you help them develop?
- What sort of play is best for learning opportunities?
- Should children under five be playing with computers?
- What skills should your child have before they start school?

Getting ready for nursery – separation anxiety
Helen Letchfield is the Co-Founder and Principal Facilitator of Parenting for Professionals, which offers individuals and companies support and coaching through maternity at work (www.parentingforprofessionals.co.uk). This is Helen's advice for how to approach your child starting at nursery, and how to minimise the (very common) phase of separation anxiety which can occur:

'Seeing your toddler's distress when you leave for a day's work can be upsetting, and hardly puts you in the right frame of mind for a happy and productive day's work! Thankfully, there are actually many things you can do to minimise the upset on both sides, and make this a positive daily event. It's also a great opportunity to boost your child's self-esteem and confidence in helping them learn to cope well with another life stage.

1. Prepare for separation early on, at home.

Playing simple games with babies and toddlers, such as 'peek-a-boo' and 'hide and seek' will help your baby understand that when he or she cannot see you, that it doesn't mean you are gone forever, but that you will return. Starting with just hiding for a few seconds will build the process slowly, and will be fun for both of you. You can also do this by putting favourite toys or teddies out of view and saying 'bye bye' and then finding them together

2. Help your child develop a new, secure 'attachment' in his or her childcare.

In order for a child to feel safe and secure, he or she needs to temporarily be able to replace the strong attachment or bond that they have with you with someone else. This is why most nurseries operate a 'key worker' system, and why it is highly recommended that you have several settling-in visits, where you stay with your toddler for long enough for them to form a relationship with their key carer. Resist the temptation to spend all the session playing with them and encourage them to find ways to interact with the carers.

If you have chosen to employ a nanny or childminder, it is clearly easier to form personal relationships quicker (that is, if you have found the right person and this will be a good test).

3. Leave positively.

How you react to leaving will have a huge impact on your toddler's behaviour. You need to give out the message loud and clear 'I am happy and relaxed about you being here'. Easier said than done in those early days, but start your leaving 'ritual' on the way over to the nursery/childminder (and as babies and toddlers thrive on routine, this is key). Talk about where you are going and what you both will do in a positive and excited way. It can also help to say the same thing each time, for example, 'I will come and pick you up after your tea and give you a big cuddle'.

When you are ready to leave, give a quick, firm hug with an 'I love you' or 'have a lovely time' and leave with a smile on your face without hesitation. It will take practice, but the carers are there to help you.

How you behave towards your child can have a big impact on how they feel about going to their childcare, so even if you do feel dreadful inside, put on the brave face for their sakes. And remember that even very young children are probably more resilient than we give them credit for, so you may find they adapt quicker to the change than you do!'
Helen Letchfield (www.parentingforprofessionals.co.uk).

What worked for us – Be consistent from home to nursery
'My daughter started nursery from nine months, initially going in just one day a week. It took her quite a long time to settle, but once she started doing three days a week she settled really quickly, loving her key workers, and currently she'll chat to everyone in her room, give cuddles, read books and is really, really happy there.

'It wasn't easy at the start, but by persevering and making her see what a fun place nursery is, her confidence grew. We're really lucky in that all the key workers are lovely and will also give us an excellent recap of everything she's done during the day.

'The one thing we've found essential with nursery is making sure we follow their guidelines – they won't use certain words (like "naughty") so H doesn't get confused signals from the two sets of people who are her primary carers (i.e. her parents and nursery) – consistency like this seems to work for us, anyway.'
Jo Brooks
Holly Blog, misshollyblog.blogspot.com

Skills your child needs by the time they start school
No matter how ready they seem to be in some ways, our under fives can still seem terribly young when they start school – as indeed they are. And even if you've resisted the lure of peer pressure so far, it's hard not to get drawn into that anxious state of fretting about how your child is going to handle school and how they'll manage alongside a larger group of children their own age.

So how far should our toddlers have progressed by the time they arrive at the pre-school stage?

For starters, don't sweat about the academic side of things – reading and writing will come in their own time at school. Many children at the reception stage are only just starting to pick up a pencil, whilst others will already be writing their own names. Whatever stage your child is at, don't worry. The teachers will tell you if there's a problem. And no, you can't change their name to a much shorter one just so they can start developing a signature.

When it comes to helping your child be ready for starting school, it's the social stuff that matters most. And this is where parents can help and make a difference. Crucially, it's not about what you do, but rather what you don't do that matters. For your pre-school child to develop the independence they need to handle school, you will need to cut back on some of the things you've done for them so far, so they develop those skills for themselves.

From around four onwards, and definitely in the summer before starting school for the first time, encourage your child in these areas:

• Dressing and undressing themselves.
Practice at home getting in and out of their P.E. kit – make sure they know that underwear is to be left on. Teachers often report a class full of nude reception children, since their only previous experience was of getting changed for bath or bed. Many schools do indoor sports with children in bare feet, so make sure your child can take their own socks on and off.

- Using the toilet alone.

If they have trouble with trouser fastenings, maybe stick to trousers with elasticated waists only for a while. Make sure they are able to wipe themselves, flush and wash their hands afterwards. Wiping can take some time for children to manage reliably, but encourage your child to at least have a go.

- Using cutlery.

Many children struggle with knives and forks, particularly if they're left-handed. If you are intending for your child to have school dinners, focus on improving these skills before the first term. Most schools will be able to give you a copy of the most recent school dinner menu if you want to see what's in store. If cutlery is really a problem, a packed lunch with sandwiches may be easier on your child for the first few weeks at least. There's a lot to learn when you start school, so minimise the pressure as much as you can.

- Opening lunchbox packets.

Schools do have extra helpers at lunchtime, but not so many that they can go round and sort out everybody's lunchbox. So think about the kind of things you intend to include and check that your child can manage them alone – can they put the straw in their juice box or pop the top off their yoghurt carton? When your child is at home, it's easy to forget how much we parents step in and help. Maybe have a few lunchbox picnics in the park to give your child some practice at sorting out their lunch by themselves.

Above all, don't panic if you think your child is nowhere near acquiring these skills. They all get there in the end and your child may just surprise you with what they can do when you give them the space to try, make mistakes, and try again. Encourage every effort and sit on your hands if you're struggling with standing back and letting them do things for themselves. It's not helping in the long run. Often the biggest barrier to a child becoming

independent is not the child themselves, but the parent who
wants to do everything for them.

Focus on fun and you'll learn through play

Teresa Bliss is a Child and Educational Psychologist and author
of several books including *Label With Care: A Book for Parents*.
This is Teresa's advice about preparing your preschooler for the
next stage:

'Personally I would not be encouraging parents to be
teaching their children reading and writing preschool unless of course the child has a natural inclination and aptitude. Parents need to be having fun with their children
and playing with them – children learn a great deal
through play.

'A minority of children are already reading before they
attend school. One of the difficulties for these children is
that they are then out of step with their peers. Doing
things orally before they sit down using pencil and paper is
far more important because this helps to develop their
attending skills, concentration and memory.

'Encourage (not pressurise) your child to recite favourite nursery rhymes. Do it together, retell parts of favourite
stories, make it fun. Retell a favourite story and get some
of the words wrong, for example, "the three little pigs"
could become the "three little wigs", instead of repeating
the familiar wolf phrase "by the hair of my chinny chin
chin" it can become "by the pair on my ninny nin pin".
When stories are very familiar and retold with little errors
children have great fun in putting you right. Again this
draws on attention, concentration, and memory – and
you're having fun with your children.

'Doing all the things above will help prepare your child
for school, and additionally lots of talk about school, reading stories about school. There are lots of good preschool
story books available that can be taken out through the

local library. Ensure that your children have rich language experiences before they go to school so that their language is as developed as possible.

'Teaching the children how to share is also important. In an affluent society a significant problem for some teachers is children's lack of experience and ability to share. Many parents buy one of each thing for their children so that they do not have to share. When children get into the school environment they have to learn to share their space, equipment and time with the teacher. Sharing is sometimes a big surprise for some children and emotionally difficult for them to manage. Teaching children how to play games and take turns as well as win or lose with grace and good manners will help. Waiting your turn and taking your turn are all things that some children find extremely difficult to manage if they have not experienced them before school.'

Teresa Bliss

www.teresabliss.com

If you are in any way concerned about how well-prepared your child is for school then talk to their nursery teacher or new primary school teacher. Your child might be more able for school than you realise – you are their first teacher and you've probably done a better job than you think.

Toddlers and technology

Technology, screen time and the online world are issues that we parents today have to think about in a way that no other generation of parents have. Should I let my toddler loose on the computer? How much screen time is too much?

I know of toddlers who have their own Facebook pages, blogs, Twitter feed and YouTube accounts. Obviously all of these are managed and produced by their parents, but they do so because they see a value in it. For the child whose family is spread out across the globe, it offers a way to share news, pictures and videos.

Skype, which lets you have video phone calls via your computer for free, can be invaluable for the pre-verbal child who lives far from their extended family. They can wave, show their latest drawing or simply play whilst their grandparents get an insight into their life and personality, no matter how far away they are. That's got to be good for long term relationships and a big step up from trying to get a child who can barely form a sentence to speak to Grandma on the phone.

I recently saw a toddler in her pram in the local shopping centre. Whilst her mum chatted to a friend, the toddler was holding an iPad in both hands and using it to watch cartoons whilst she lay back in her buggy. Reports from the US suggest that this is becoming a more and more common sight.

Some of you may be taken aback by this, whilst others who eagerly adopt the latest technology may see it as the natural evolution of our age. Or maybe it's a sign that we have become too casual with how we treat expensive bits of tech. But whether you agree with it or not, there is no denying that our children are growing up in a technology-reliant society, and that isn't going to change. What is changing is how they interact with that technology, and how often they do it.

Should a toddler be using a computer?

Chances are, if they're at nursery they already are, and even if they haven't used a computer at home, they will be aware that such things exist. Technology is developing at a frightening pace, but that doesn't mean we have to be scared of it. Your child may be doing things with computers at primary school that the previous generation would only have encountered at university. It's exciting as much as it's amazing.

What works for us – A mixture of tech and traditional
Ruth blogs at Geek Mummy and has two children under five:
'We have a lot of technology in the house – iPads, iPhones, computers, laptops. Even our television – we use an Apple Mac Mini instead of a Sky box or similar.

'We have a very relaxed attitude to our kids and technology. We try to not treat it as anything special, but rather a tool or a toy to be used in balance with everything else. We do monitor their screen time, and try to keep within the official guidelines of 1-2 hours per day, although I tend to not class time spent playing with educational apps on the iPad as screen time in the same way as I can see the huge benefit my daughter gets from it.

'Catherine has been able to operate our iPad and iPhone from about the age of two – that means switching it on, navigating to the app she wants, selecting it and then playing it. I have been pleasantly surprised at how much she enjoys educational apps – for example ones that allow her to trace numbers or letters on the screen – as well as games like matching or jigsaws. She also enjoys browsing through the family photos and videos as well.

'My daughter was born the year the first iPhone launched, my son was born two days after the first iPad went on sale – they're growing up with this technology, and have never known life without it. A funny example of this – we went into a shop selling toys, and in one corner was a very tiny TV screen playing a DVD – Catherine walked up to the screen and tried to use the two finger pinch you'd use on an iPad to make the picture bigger!

'I don't think tech toys (certainly not at this age) push away traditional toys. My daughter loves colouring in, and reading books, and whilst we have iPad apps for both of these things, she prefers the traditional form. She also loves playing outside and we just got her one of those giant trampoline things which she adores. It's all a ques-

tion of balance – if she started only being interested in the tech toys I would become more prescriptive about when she could or could not play with them.'
Geekmummy.com

It's all about balance
While computer-based play can have benefits for the under fives, it needs to exist within a balance of other activities, particularly physical activity. No sense in knowing your way round the app store if you don't have the energy to go to the real store.

So use your common sense – it's great if a child has an aptitude for technology, but that should never edge out other forms of play, particularly playing with other children.

It works for us – technology with limits
Ellie Hirsch is the mother of two boys and founder of *Mommy Masters*:
'My boys, aged four and two, are well aware of the gaming options out there and recently asked for me to buy them their own iPad. Borrowing Daddy's new iPad simply isn't enough and they want to be able to log on at their leisure. It really amazes me that my two year old can understand how to find a game, click on it, start it up and begin playing, all by himself. He understands the concept of touching, dragging, clicking, pushing, moving and every other instruction needed to win. These skills will play a role in how my children and yours learn in the future, and will provide them with a head start as new technology develops along with them. You will be happy to know I declined their request for a new iPad and heavily regulate their online playtime.

'We all know at times our kids need distractions, and all these high tech possessions are great tools for parents to utilize in certain situations, such as doctor's waiting rooms, airports, shopping trips or rainy days. On the flip side though, one has to hope that parents can set limits as to what is acceptable play time and when it's time to shut down. We have to allow children to be children, letting them run outside getting fresh air or playing inside, completing puzzles or building with good old blocks; not permitting them to be a slave to an entertainment device.

'Whether it's a tablet, cell phone or computer, our children are extremely lucky they can take advantage of such amazing technology at such a young age, and I feel there is high educational value in allowing a child technological access. They are learning while playing, which to me is a wonderful philosophy and shared by many pre-school programs in the country. Allow your child to explore, learn and have fun, but set limits. It's an exciting time for them and who knows what is coming their way next!'

Ellie Hirsch

www.mommymasters.blogspot.com

Educational play ideas to prepare for school

Whilst tech toys are on the rise, classic play is still here to stay. So if you're choosing toys for your child, especially if you want them to have some sort of educational benefits, remember that the simpler something is, the more a child has to bring their imagination to it. This is why something like a giant cardboard box can be one of the most fun things to play with and why classic toys like building blocks and dolls have stood the test of time and will continue to endure.

Remember that you don't have to spend a fortune on your toddler to help them have a good time. In fact, they'd probably get overwhelmed (as would your house) if you did.

Be led by your child in terms of their interests. Read to them every day, but be prepared for them not to want to sit still to hear the whole of the story. Children of this age often like the same story repeatedly – tough luck if it's one you're sick of already.

Give your child access to chunky crayons, but don't be concerned if they're not ready to pick them up yet. Any toy which encourages fine motor skills (small movements of the hands and fingers) will, eventually, help them to develop writing skills. This includes:

- Sewing games – either a printed sewing card that you thread with a shoelace, or make your own by threading a cotton reel or some dried penne pasta and a piece of string;
- Painting – use a big brush and stand well back to admire the most abstract creations you ever did see;
- Drawing in the sand – either with a finger, paintbrush or chopstick.

Can you see how any of these games will encourage your child to make a connection between what they're doing with their hands and what they can see with their eyes? This will one day lead them to be able to write.

Above all, don't sweat it. Your child has a long, long time in education in front of them. As they grow older and their personality develops, there will be certain characteristics that will stay – the pouty look when they're tired, or the unwillingness to deal easily with change or share their food.

But mostly, your child is like a flower opening its petals right now. This is not all they can be, it's who they are becoming. Just because they run away from books now doesn't mean they won't become an avid reader. Just because they won't hold a crayon doesn't mean they won't one day write a novel.

Be aware of the next phase, but also enjoy where you and your child are right now. You'll miss it when it's gone.

Key points about starting school or nursery:
- You can minimise separation anxiety;
- Computers can be of value to toddlers, but mix it up with traditional play too;

- Don't fret about the academic side of school – you will help your child much more if you concentrate on social skills.

What I love about my pre-schooler
'From baby days of drool and spit, and mostly nappies and shhhh…, suddenly there is a small human being standing in front of me and giving me lip. From arguments about why breakfast isn't quite what she feels like this morning and a long discussion as to why her room actually IS very tidy, this little person is suddenly very much there. Know what I mean? Her two feet are being firmly stood upon as she locks my eyes in a gimlet gaze and pushes every single button I have. She could have tidied both her room and the lounge in the time it took her to argue against doing it but that isn't going to stop her doing it over and over again. And you know what? I love it. I love her mad moments and her arguments, I love her mini tantrums and her stubborn glares and most of all I adore those soft, soft, soft seconds when she curls up in my arms and lets me breathe her in. And then she proceeds to find something new to argue about…

'I'm not going to lie. It drives me completely insane. However, it is so utterly real and typical of her age that it almost makes me proud. She's hitting those benchmarks and ticking those developmental boxes so I must be doing something right and that's a huge relief. I may scour the internet and bookshops for expert guidance but it is still down to my husband and I to get things right and these moments make me feel like we're not completely screwing things up.'
Tamsin Oxford
Saffa So Good, saffasogood.com

Why I love my toddlers, even the ones who've grown up
'Eowyn will soon be three and I love the fact that she makes me feel special, no matter what. Last week when I was colouring my hair and had a head full of red gunk, she came up to me and said 'Oh Mummy you look so blooti-ful!' (She hasn't quite got 'beautiful'!)

'When Kaide was a toddler he did THE most groovy dancing. I love the way that toddlers do not care about what is going on around them, when they are in their own little "zone" nothing else matters, and the break dancing was so cool!

'When Neva was a toddler I had lost my bank cards. I asked her if she had seen them and she said 'Yes'. She then spent the next half an hour taking me on a tour of our house saying "I put them here Mummy", which of course she hadn't. I eventually found them, buried inside one of her little handbags that was inside another, and another…You have to love them no matter what!

'Toddlers have this amazing ability to sleep anywhere! Lochlan could literally sleep on a dance floor. And in the winter I can remember Lochlan dressed in a padded green snowsuit throwing himself into the snow, literally belly flopping, hilarious to watch, with complete disregard for his own safety.

'Most of all I love their new found independence once they reach this age. Up until then I had happily chosen Xene's clothes to wear each day, when all of a sudden she decided she would much rather choose her own! Some of the combinations that came out of that wardrobe were a little questionable, however I am happy to say that now she's a teenager she has great taste in clothes.'
Mandi Morrison, mother of six
Hex Mum, hexmum.blogspot.com

Useful contacts and other resources

Useful books:

1 2 3 Magic: Effective Discipline for Children, Thomas Phelan

Blogging for happiness – A guide to improving positive mental health (and wealth) from your blog, Ellen Arnison

Cool, Calm Parent – How not to lose it with your kids, Hollie Smith

Dealing With Difficult Eaters, Dr Sandi Mann, Hollie Smith and Sally Child

Down to Earth With a Bump – The Diary of a First Time Dad, Andrew Watson

How to Talk so Kids Will Listen and Listen so Kids Will Talk, Adele Faber and Elaine Mazlish

Label With Care – A Book for Parents, Teresa Bliss

Toddler Taming, Dr Christopher Green

Toddling to Ten – Hollie Smith

What *to Expect – The Toddler Years*, Arlene Eisenberg, Heidi E. Murkoff and Sandee E. Hathaway

Useful websites:

www.bloggered.co.uk
www.britmums.com
www.firstwayforward.com
www.Kidz4Mation.com
www.lunchboxworld.com
www.mum-friendly.co.uk
www.Mumsnet.com
www.NetMums.com
www.parentingforprofessionals.co.uk
www.relaxkids.com
www.singlewithkids.co.uk

Thank you everyone who helped in the preparation of this book, especially those of you who contributed your precious time and valuable words:

Alex – *Little Miss Madam and the Sunshine Duke*,
    www.littlemissmadamandthesunshineduke.blogspot.com
Alex Walsh – *Daddacool*, www.daddacool.co.uk
Almost Bedtime, www.12hourstobedtime.blogspot.com
Andrew Watson – www.awwa.co.uk
Angela Cheung – *This is Life*, www.angela-
    thisislife.blogspot.com
Angeline Brunel – *Daft Mamma*, www.daftmamma.co.uk
Anya Harris – *Older Single Mum*,
    www.oldersinglemum.blogspot.com
BareNaked Mummy, www.barenakedmummy.blogspot.com
Bob – *Wisdom Begins in Wonder*,
    www.wisdombeginsinwonder.com
Boo – *Boo, Roo and Tigger Too*,
    www.boorootiggertoo.blogspot.com
Caroline Job – *Lunchbox World*, www.lunchboxworld.com
Cathy James – *NurtureStore*, www.nurturestore.co.uk
Christine Lewandowski – *Single With Kids*,
    www.singlewithkids.co.uk
Elaine – *Fun-as-a-Gran*, www.fun-as-a-gran.blogspot.com
Ella Tabb – *Purple Mum*, www.purplemum.com
Ellen Arnison – *In A Bun Dance*, www.bundance.blogspot.com
Ellie Hirsch – *Mommy Masters*,
    www.mommymasters.blogspot.com
Emily Carlisle – *More Than Just a Mother*,
    www.morethanjustamother.com
Emma – *Mummy Musings*, www.mummymusings.co.uk
Hazel Gaynor – *Hot Cross Mum*,
    www.hotcrossmum.blogspot.com
Heather Young – *Young & Younger*, www.youngandyounger.net
Heidi Scrimgeour – www.heidiscrimgeour.com

Helen Letchfield – *Parenting for Professionals*,
    www.parentingforprofessionals.co.uk
Helen Redfern – www.helenredfern.com
Janice Thompson – *A Working Mum*, www.aworkingmum.com
Jo Brooks – *Holly Blog*, www.misshollyblog.blogspot.com
Jo Waters – www.jowaters.co.uk/blog.html
Josephine Middleton – *Slummy Single Mummy*,
    www.slummysinglemummy.wordpress.com
Kate – *Life, Love and Living With Boys*,
    www.lifeloveandlivingwithboys.wordpress.com
Kay – *Brink of Bedlam*, www.brinkofbedlam.co.uk
Kizzy Bass – *Mummy Needs...*,
    www.mummyneeds.wordpress.com
Kylie Hodges – *Not even a bag of sugar*,
    www.notevena.blogspot.com
Laura Nelson – *The Breastest News*, www.thebreastestnews.co.uk
Lauren Goodchild – *The Wonderful Adventures of Spud and Spike*,
    www.spudandspike.co.uk
Lisha Aquino Rooney – *Oomphalos*, www.oomphalos.co.uk
Lynda Hudson – www.firstwayforward.com
Mandi Morrison – *Hex Mum*, www.hexmum.blogspot.com
Maria Jose Ovalle – *Mummy's Busy World*,
    www.mummysbusyworld.com
Marneta Viegas – www.relaxkids.com
Michelle Hanlon – www.michellehanlon.blogspot.com
Nadine Hill – *Juggle Mum*, www.jugglemum.com
Natalie Donohoe – *Livi Lou & Dude*,
    www.liviloudude.blogspot.com
Nicki Cawood – *Curly and Candid*, www.curlyandcandid.co.uk
Nicola Seary – *Comp Chat and Kids*,
    www.compchatandkids.wordpress.com
Paula Fazekas – *Mummy vs Work*, www.mummyvswork.co.uk
Rachel McClary – *Right From the Start*,
    www.rightfromthestart.wordpress.com
Ramblings of a Suburban Mummy, www.realsuburbanmummy.com
Ruth – *Geekmummy*, www.geekmummy.com

Sarah Cruickshank – www.sarahcruickshank.co.uk
Seema Thobhani – www.kidz4mantion.com
Sian – *You're Not From Round Here*,
    www.offcumden.blogspot.com
Spencer – *SAHD and Proud*,
    www.sahdandproud.wordpress.com
Susie Newday – *New day, New lesson*,
    www.newdaynewlesson.com
Tamsin Oxford – *Saffa So Good*, www.saffasogood.com
Tania Sullivan – *Larger Family Life*, www.largerfamilylife.com
Tarryn Hunt – *Mums That Care*, www.MumsThatCare.com
Teresa Bliss – www.teresabliss.com
Tim Atkinson – *Bringing Up Charlie*,
    www.bringingupcharlie.co.uk
Tracy Cazaly – *Family, Parents, Girls, Devon*,
    www.familyparentsgirlsdevon.blogspot.com
Ursula Hirschkorn – *Four Down, Mum to Go*,
    www.fourdownmumtogo.blogspot.com
Wendy – *Mum in Awe*, www.muminawe.com

Index